ZERO
Fighter

Mitsubishi Zero Fighter Model 52, A6M5 (Drawing by Suzuki Yukio)

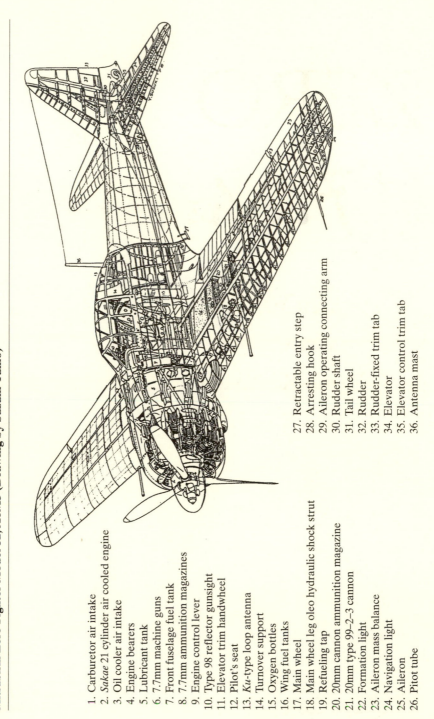

1. Carburetor air intake
2. *Sakae* 21 cylinder air cooled engine
3. Oil cooler air intake
4. Engine bearers
5. Lubricant tank
6. 7.7mm machine guns
7. Front fuselage fuel tank
8. 7.7mm ammunition magazines
9. Engine control lever
10. Type 98 reflector gunsight
11. Elevator trim handwheel
12. Pilot's seat
13. *Ku*-type loop antenna
14. Turnover support
15. Oxygen bottles
16. Wing fuel tanks
17. Main wheel
18. Main wheel leg oleo hydraulic shock strut
19. Refueling tap
20. 20mm cannon ammunition magazine
21. 20mm type 99–2–3 cannon
22. Formation light
23. Aileron mass balance
24. Navigation light
25. Aileron
26. Pitot tube
27. Retractable entry step
28. Arresting hook
29. Aileron operating connecting arm
30. Rudder shaft
31. Tail wheel
32. Rudder
33. Rudder-fixed trim tab
34. Elevator
35. Elevator control trim tab
36. Antenna mast

ZERO
Fighter

Akira Yoshimura

TRANSLATED BY

Retsu Kaiho and Michael Gregson

Westport, Connecticut
London

Library of Congress Cataloging-in-Publication Data

Yoshimura, Akira.
   [Reishiki sentōki. English]
   Zero fighter / Akira Yoshimura ; translated by Retsu Kaiho and
Michael Gregson.
     p.   cm.
   Includes index.
   ISBN 0–275–95355–6 (alk. paper)
   1. Zero (Fighter planes). I. Title.
UG1242.F5Y6713   1996
940.54'4952—dc20   95–19744

British Cataloguing in Publication Data is available.

Library of Congress Catalog Card Number: 95–19744
ISBN: 0–275–95355–6

First published in 1996

Praeger Publishers, 88 Post Road West, Westport, CT 06881
An imprint of Greenwood Publishing Group, Inc.

This book was designed and typeset by Letra Libre,
1705 14th Street, Suite 391, Boulder, CO 80302

Printed in the United States of America

The paper used in this book complies with the
Permanent Paper Standard issued by the National
Information Standards Organization (Z39.48–1984).

10 9 8 7 6 5 4 3 2 1

For our friend, Shingen Nagaoka

One

Just after 7 P.M. on March 23, 1939, two oxcarts emerged from the gates of the Nagoya Aircraft Works of Mitsubishi Heavy Industries, Ltd. Each cart was heavily laden with a large cargo shrouded in canvas. Slowly the carts moved north, following the street car tracks along the main street of the city of Nagoya.

The oxcarts belonged to the Onishi company, contracted for this job by the Nagoya works of Mitsubishi. The two drivers holding the bridles of the oxen each held a lantern in his hand. Written in bold letters on those lanterns was the name of the Onishi company, under the ensign of the Mitsubishi company, which was three diamonds. Four heavers paced alongside the carts, guarding the loads. At the head of the ponderous little procession walked Seiichiro Tamura, transportation supervisor of the materials section of the aircraft works. A security guard brought up the rear.

The drivers and heavers had an idea of what was on the carts. The front one was loaded with an airplane's wings and the front part of its fuselage. The second cart carried the after part of the fuselage with a horizontal stabilizer and an engine section. The teamsters knew this because it was routine to disassemble a completed airplane into wings and fuselages for transport to the Kagamigahara Airfield of Gifu

Prefecture, forty-eight kilometers away. Transportation companies such as Onishi, Murase, Higashiyama, Tsue, and Kato were regularly employed to make the trip there. On this night, however, the drivers and heavers had a vague awareness that the load on their oxcarts was of unusual importance. This is because Tamura, the transport supervisor, would not otherwise be accompanying them.

Only Tamura knew that the load was a newly developed plane, manufactured for the navy at the airframe factory of the first manufacturing division of the navy. Tamura had directed the loading of the parts by crane onto the carts and seen that they belonged to a new fighter.

The oxcarts moved along the main street. On the uneven, stony road, the iron-rimmed wheels ground and rattled loudly. The loads swayed heavily. Progress was slow. It would take twenty-four hours, including a few hours for a rest, to cover the forty-eight kilometers to the airfield.

It seems astonishing that a modern, high-speed fighter should be carried to its test field on an oxcart, but despite objections, the Nagoya Aircraft Works had no other choice. In the first place, the Nagoya works had no adjoining airfield of its own. An airfield needed a vast site and the land simply was not available. As the Nagoya factory of the Aichi Aircraft Company and the Himeji factory of the Kawanishi Aircraft Company also had no fields, however, the Mitsubishi plant did not feel badly about this lack. Then there was the fact that methods of transportation alternative to oxcarts had proved inadequate.

Trucks had been tried. A truck took only two hours to cover the distance to the Kagamigahara Airfield. Out of Nagoya, however, the roads were so rough that aircraft carried on trucks had been damaged by strong shocks and vibrations. Horse drawn carts had also been tried. Horses made the trip in twelve hours. But the possibility of stampede made it too risky to entrust delicate aircraft fuselages to horses.

The narrowness of the road in parts also created problems for travel by means other than oxcart. In the town of Komaki, halfway along the route, the loads grazed the eaves of houses as they passed between, and once a large bomber had been damaged trying to negotiate Komaki's narrow streets. In the transport of aircraft, avoiding damage was the first priority, and in the circumstances, only the slowness of an oxcart offered an acceptable margin of safety. Tradition added some dignity to the oxcart, besides. During the Heian period (eighth–twelfth centuries, when the emperor had directly governed) nobles themselves had travelled in oxcarts, the least bumpy on the rough roads.

As the carts creaked through Nagoya, they passed in front of the east gate of the Atsuta shrine. Tamura and the guard stopped there and made a bow before resuming their posts at the front and rear of the procession. The party went over the Kanayama Bridge, crossed the streetcar tracks and with a great squeaking and rattling of the heavily loaded wheels, turned north. A street car flashing electricity from its trolley pole came from the rear and passed them. Tsurumai Park came up on the right side.

Tamura wiped his sweaty forehead with a towel and looked at his wristwatch in the dim light of a driver's lantern. It was turning 9 P.M.

They passed the cross at Shinei. Nunobike Block drew near. The eyes of Tamura and the guard became fixed on the nearest Western-style building on the right side of the road.

The journey was being made by night not just to avoid the high traffic density of the day in Nagoya. There were strong security concerns, too. As few people as possible were to set eyes on the newly developed aircraft, and as part of the precautions, the navy's supervisor at the Nagoya Aircraft Works had instructed the police to take up station at proper points all along the route. Many police watched silently from the shadows as the procession passed along. The greatest danger, however, was a disturbing rumor at the aircraft works that the windows of the U.S. Consulate at Nunobiki were almost always open slightly when oxcarts loaded with planes passed by. With diplomatic relations between the United States and Japan deteriorating, it was known that the Americans took a very serious view of military developments in Japan, and must be doing their best to gather information.

Under these circumstances, it was considered a grave risk to pass in front of the consulate, and once the route had even been changed to avoid the place. But it was found that there were passersby on every street, even at night. Also it was felt a sudden change of route might attract the notice of the consulate. So the old route was resumed.

As Tamura passed he watched the consulate's darkened rows of windows with a stiff expression. None were open.

Just after midnight, the carts passed through Osone and came out of Nagoya. From here the road became narrow and its condition extremely bad. They crossed the Sankai Bridge over the Yada River and the Mikumari Bridge, rattling its girders. Though they had been on the move since just after 7 P.M., a steady pace was kept up. A young moon came up in a sky of dim stars.

In the predawn hours, the carts began to encounter a traffic of trucks and horse-carts jolting along the bad road. Tamura swung his lantern and shouted "Military Transportation! Give us priority on the road!" to make the oncoming traffic yield.

The whiteness of dawn had replaced night's blackness, and the lanterns had been blown out when the party at last reached the verge of Komaki, halfway point on the twenty-four hour journey. Here they took a brief rest. The oxen were given fodder while the men had a bowl of rice at an eating house under contract. The oxen were rested for about three hours. Then the party started for Inuyama.

All day, Tamura used a red flag to clear a way through oncoming traffic. The creaking, swaying loads progressed steadily, and the sun was declining in the west when they came at last to Inuyama. There they took another rest before treading a road flooded with evening sunshine toward Kagamigahara Airfield. Darkness was upon them by the time they saw the lights of that place.

The vast Kagamigahara Airfield was divided into three sections. The eastern one, facing the Kiso River, was used and controlled by the Second Air Regiment of the army. The western part, on the side of Gifu was run by the First Air Regiment. The intermediate section of the airfield was run by the Kagamigahara Branch of the supply department of the Aeronautical Headquarters of the army. It was between the gate poles of the supply department that the oxcarts passed. They stopped in front of the hangar used by the Nagoya Aircraft Works.

Engineers and workers, brought in from the aircraft works by the train, were on hand to help the hangar ground crew unload and assemble the aircraft. Work began at once. In the midst of it, the headlights of the truck carrying parts from the Oe factory appeared shining in the dark.

The off-loading was completed quickly. Then the oxcarts were disassembled and put aboard the truck along with the teamsters and their oxen. They drove away and assembly of the aircraft began.

The ground crew of the hangar helping engineers and workers from the Oe factory were immediately curious about the wing made of shining duralumin that appeared from under the cover of canvas. They said nothing, however, as many other features they had never seen in a fighter aircraft came to their eye. It was bigger than conventional planes; it had a fuselage that was slim and graceful. The wings were unusually thin. The wheels were retractable. As the assembly progressed, the men worked in silent astonishment at this really new creature of the air.

Two

This newly developed fighter was the fruit of long years of research by the Aeronautical Department of Mitsubishi Heavy Industries, Ltd. It was also the plane that had overcome the short history of the aeronautical industry in Japan.

The first flights in Japan were made on December 19, 1912, by Captain Yoshitoshi Tokugawa and Captain Kumazo Hino. Captain Tokugawa flew for about four minutes, or 3,000 meters, in a French Henri Farman biplane. Captain Hino flew one minute and twenty seconds, or about 1,200 meters, in a German Grade monoplane. Aeronautics in Japan, however, remained at the stage of importing foreign planes and learning how to pilot them until 1916 or 1917. In the fifteen years that followed, until 1930 or 1931, aeronautics moved onto the stage of making foreign planes under license. Foreign engineers were invited to design aircraft and supervise production of airframes and engines.

In the military sphere, the first carrier-borne fighter of the Nagoya works of Mitsubishi was produced in October 1921. This plane, piloted by Lieutenant Shunichi Kira, succeeded in landing on the deck of the aircraft carrier *Hosho* (Flying Phoenix) for the first time in the Japanese navy on March 16, 1923. The plane had been designed by

Smith, an engineer invited from England. Smith had formerly worked for the British Sopwith Aircraft Company. The engine was a foreign one, made under license by Mitsubishi.

Japan's shipbuilding capability was first class in terms of the world and well able to produce the "8-8 Fleet" project of the navy (the "8-8" plan called for eight battle cruisers and eight battleships to form the nucleus of Japan's fleet). Compared to shipbuilding, however, aeronautics was at a level of development far inferior to aeronautics in Europe and North America. Reliance on foreign designers for planes was great.

It was the designs of Smith and others that guided Mitsubishi in producing the Type 10 carrier-borne fighter, Type 10 carrier-borne reconnaissance plane, and the Type 10 carrier-borne torpedo-bomber. At the army's request, the company's Nagoya works also produced the French Nieuport trainer under a production license purchased from the Anrio Aircraft Company.

The move toward all-metal aircraft in Japan started after the end of World War I in 1918. Until then, airplanes were commonly made of wood or a combination of wood and metal. During the war, however, Germany had developed the lightweight metal duralumin, and used it to construct the gigantic Zeppelin airships and strutless monoplanes. The material captured the attention of the aeronautical world, and after the 1918 armistice, the Allies, including Japan, obtained the production license for duralumin. Interest in an all-metal airplane developed rapidly.

In Japan, Dr. Aikitsu Tanakadate, the country's leading authority on aeronautics, was key in influencing the navy's aeronautical staff to pursue the development of an all metal plane. The navy began by engaging a German engineer, Rohrbach, to build a factory in Copenhagen, Denmark and design and build for it an all-metal flying boat, the Type R. In May 1922, the navy also sent to Germany a team of engineers and helpers to learn to construct all-metal aircraft. Lieutenant Misao Wada, who had been studying aeronautics at the University of Tokyo, led the navy group, which consisted of two other engineers, Tetsuo Noda and Junichiro Nagahata, two engineering aids, and sixteen workers. The army and Mitsubishi also sent staff with Wada to Germany—Sato and another engineer for the army, Keisuke Otsuka and Joji Hattori for Mitsubishi. At the same time, a group also went to Germany to study the production of duralumin. This group was headed by Captain Ishikawa of the navy, and included an engineer, Fujii, from the Sumitomo Metal Company.

In 1924, during his stay in Germany, Lieutenant Wada got Rohrbach to produce four more of the Type R flying boat, an all-metal twin-engine monoplane, after the prototype was made at the new factory in Copenhagen. Also, one Type R flying boat was constructed at Mitsubishi under the direction of Rohrbach.

After returning to Japan, Wada, who had been promoted to commander, designed an all-metal flying boat, the Type 90 Model 1, based on study of Rohrbach's Type R ship. It was built at the Hiro Naval Yard with some assistance from Rear Admiral Yuzuru Hiraga, a naval architect. The navy officially adopted this aircraft and produced six.

It was from this time that naval aircraft of wholly Japanese design and manufacture began to appear. Early designs included the Type 3 Model 2 ground-based primary trainer (by the Yokosuka Naval Yard), the Type 89 flying boat (by the Hiro Naval Yard), the Type 90 operation trainer (by Mitsubishi), and the Type 90 carrier-borne fighter. However, there still remained a tendency to rely upon the aeronautical technology of foreign countries, partly because Japan had a great deal of catching up to do yet.

This tendency became very apparent in the 1926 competition for a new carrier-borne fighter. The navy ordered three companies to take part: Aichi, Nakajima, and Mitsubishi. They had a year to come up with a design. Having monopolized the design of all Japanese carrier-borne planes up to that time, Mitsubishi had great self-confidence in its submission, which owed a great deal to its Type 10 fighter. The navy, however, judged the Nakajima design—an almost direct copy of the Gampet carrier-borne fighter made by the Gloucester company of Britain—to be the best, and this plane was adopted.

The navy's choice had a strong effect on the industry, and in the 1928 competition for a carrier-borne torpedo bomber, a reliance on foreign design showed up even more strongly. This time the victor was Mitsubishi.

Mitsubishi had taken its 1926 loss to Nakajima hard and felt that in the torpedo bomber race, its face was at stake. After all, ever since the creation of its Type 13 model, Mitsubishi had also monopolized the manufacture of the navy's torpedo bombers. The company determined to win the torpedo bomber competition by fair means or foul. This meant giving up its own design and adopting the Nakajima company's approach, which was to ask foreign companies for the fundamental designs. Mitsubishi approached the British Blackburn company, Handley Page, and the British engineer Herbert Smith and submitted their designs to the Navy. Blackburn's was selected. Mitsubishi constructed a prototype. This was adopted by the navy as the Type 89 carrier-borne torpedo bomber.

The navy would have preferred to use Japanese-designed planes, but it had no choice. Its aircraft were already involved in the conflict in China, and in actual battle conditions, only the superior performer was acceptable. The outcome of the 1926 and 1928 competitions, however, did little to encourage a commitment to originality in manufacturers. Then, almost overnight, the trend to foreign design was reversed.

The Shanghai Incident of 1932 jolted the navy awake to the importance of the air war. At the insistence of two senior officers, Vice Admiral Masatake Anto, second director of the Aeronautical Headquarters, and Commander Tadatake Sakurai, chief of staff of the engineering department of Naval Headquarters, the navy began to work urgently toward establishing independence in Japanese aeronautics.

As a first step, the navy formed the Aeronautical Establishment at a site adjoining the base of the Yokosuka Naval Corps on April 11, 1931. This was done even before the end of the Shanghai Incident. Vice Admiral Yuriichi Edahara was assigned first director. Edahara then set about the task of injecting new enthusiasm for original design among the companies. This process culminated in a meeting called by Edahara at the Aeronautical Establishment with the designers of each type of aircraft produced by the companies.

Edahara presented them with a new incentive, the "7Si" (Seventh Development Project), which had just been announced by the government. The project, Edahara told them, was a first step in the development of independent aeronautical technology for the navy, and the results would have far-reaching implications for aviation throughout Japan. Then he announced five aircraft design competitions. One of them was for a new carrier-borne fighter. Edahara emphasized that only designs based on Japanese research would be acceptable in these competitions.

Of the companies competing for the new carrier-borne fighter, Mitsubishi in particular was enthusiastic about the call for original design. The company had a history of designing its own planes. Now the competition offered a chance to really prove the worth of this approach against the Nakajima company, which had won the 1926 fighter competition using a foreign design.

For this intense contest, the heads of the Nagoya Aircraft Works decided to appoint as chief designer Jiro Horikoshi, an engineer already working in the design section. Those delegated to assist him included Eitaro Sano, Takanosuke Nakamura, Tomio Kubo, Fukuizumi Hatanaka, and Setsuji Fukunaga, among others.

Horikoshi was a young man for his position. He had graduated from the Department of Aeronautics in the School of Engineering at Tokyo Imperial University only five years before his appointment and was less than thirty years old. He was regarded highly, however, for his absolute commitment to his chosen field and his carefulness—he was not a man to tolerate small errors. In his favor also was a wide experience with design, especially airframe design, gained on visits to manufacturers in other countries, and in particular Junkers in Germany and Curtiss in America. Even so, however, Horikoshi had never headed a design team, and at first he was at a loss in the face of the great responsibilities of his position.

Part of the daunting quality of Horikoshi's mission was that the navy had given no official instructions for the structure or configuration of the new fighter. That left him to make the most basic decisions, for which he would have to take full responsibility. The situation made Horikoshi lonely and filled him with deep worry about his lack of design experience, and his position was not made any easier by the navy's performance requirements for the new fighter:

- Maximum climb speed: 325–375 km/hour
- Climb rate: 3,000 meters within four minutes
- Wing span: smaller than 10.3 meters

These requirements were considerably higher than those demanded of the fighters operating in China at the time. The Type 90 carrier fighter (a biplane design) with which Nakajima had won the 1926 fighter competition, was required to have a speed of 280 kilometers per hour and be able to reach 3,000 meters in five minutes 45 seconds. The other plane in combat use, the army's Type 91 aircraft (a parasol type monoplane) was required to make a top speed of 300 kilometers per hour.

At the time Horikoshi was trying to decide what configuration to adopt for the plane, the biplane was the most common design among the world's fighters, with a few parasol type monoplanes also beginning to appear. There were some excellent designs among these aircraft, but Horikoshi judged that these types would come to their limits soon.

The idea of using a mono-wing was suggested to him by Commander Jiro Saba, who was on the staff of the newly founded Aeronautical Establishment. Saba recommended a new type of low monowing, an inverse gull type, the lowest points of which were tied with a horizontal strut. Horikoshi began research on this suggestion, but then began to think that a strutless low mono-wing configuration was simpler and more promising.

His decision to adopt a low mono-wing configuration was a considerable risk for him to take. There was plenty of research and examples of flights available on biplanes and parasol type monoplanes. On strutless mono-wings, there was very little. A tremendous amount of research would have to be done from scratch. Only the creative desire of Horikoshi's team and the support of the company made Mitsubishi accept the risk in adopting a strutless low-wing configuration, but once they started, their originality extended also to many more details of the fighter's structure.

On March 8, 1933, the number one prototype of Horikoshi's new fighter was ready. It looked clumsy and unbalanced, but the low monowing configuration gave the impression to people that somehow it had potential. Company pilots Yoshitaka Kajima and Sumitoshi Nakajima began test flights at once.

At about the same time, the Nakajima company's prototype was also ready for testing. Nakajima's plane was developed from the army's Type 91 fighter, a biplane. When tried against the Mitsubishi design, the Nakajima plane was more maneuverable, Mitsubishi's a little faster. Neither plane, however, came up to performance requirements. Both were disqualified.

This discouraging result was followed immediately by the crash of the prototype. During a diving test at Kagamigahara Airfield, the vertical tail plane suddenly broke. Pilot Yoshitaka Kajima managed to bail out safely, but the plane, circling by itself, as if to avoid houses and fields and forests, finally glided to a crash landing on a beach of the Kiso River.

Though the number one plane had been destroyed, the navy, impressed by its originality, made Mitsubishi produce another, and at the Aeronautical Establishment next to Yokosuka Airfield subjected this second prototype to its own tests. Unfortunately, this prototype too was lost. While pilot Lieutenant Motoharu Okamura was trying a flight test, the aircraft went from a double roll to a horizontal spin and could not recover. Okamura lost four fingers of his left hand from touching the propeller as he bailed out, but landed safely.

Despite these crashes, however, the navy was impressed, and it was considered that much had been learned about the performance of low mono-wings from the prototypes.

As a whole, the Seventh Development Project, calling for the creation of five new types of planes, had produced few successes. Only the Kawanishi company's three-seater sea scout plane had come up to performance requirements. All others had been disqualified, including the long-range twin-engine land-based torpedo bomber (another all-metal monoplane), which had been proposed by Rear Admiral Yamamoto and Captain Wada.

By the start of 1934, the low mono-wing configuration had become the trend in all twin-engine, metal planes of bigger than medium size around the world, and performances were showing a rapid improvement. Faced with this development, the navy determined to renew its drive to create independence in Japanese aeronautical capability. The means chosen was the 9-Si (Ninth Development Project).

Begun in 1934, the Ninth Development Project was to continue development of all planes that had not succeeded during the Seventh Development Project. Among these was the new carrier-borne fighter. Again the contest for this craft was between Mitsubishi and Nakajima. This time, however, reference to the fighter as "carrier-borne" was left out of the requirements. Instead it was called a "single-seat fighter." Behind this change of label was a determination to force designers to concentrate on the new plane's performance in the air as a fighter, without concern for takeoff and landing capabilities. In pursuit of this aim, the conditions governing takeoff and landing capability were left out of the specifications.

The requirements given the competing companies were simple:

- Maximum speed: more than 350 kilometers per hour at 3,000 meters.
- Climbing rate: less than six minutes thirty seconds to 5,000 meters.
- Range: more than 200 liters of fuel capacity (for fixed tank; engine assumed to be 600-horsepower class).
- Armaments and equipment: two sets of 7.7-millimeter fixed machine guns, radio receiver only.
- Dimensional restriction: less than eleven meters in width, less than eight meters in length.

At its Nagoya Aircraft Works Mitsubishi assigned twenty to thirty engineers to this fighter project. Again Jiro Horikoshi headed up the team.

Tomio Kubo, Yoshitoshi Sone, and Yoshio Yoshikawa were responsible for the strength of the structure. Shokichi Mizuno and Hisamitsu Shimizu had charge of the power plant. Fukuizumi Hatanaka, Yoichi Ohashi, and Hideo Koda dealt with armaments and equipment. Toshitake Hirose took on the job of general manager and chief of the maintenance crew. They set to work feverishly, building on the design philosophy and experience gained with the prototypes of the Seventh Development Project.

The fundamental thrusts in the new design were to reduce air resistance and make the plane as light as possible. In pursuit of these characteristics, Horikoshi decided to depart from usual practice up till then and use a flush protruding rivet instead of a round one on the exterior surfaces of the airframe. Horikoshi had been concerned about the resistance created by the numerous rivets that protruded on the surface of an aircraft. When he discussed the problem with a fellow engineer, Suero Honjo, Honjo showed Horikoshi a drawing of a flush rivet obtained from the Junkers Company of Germany. The rivet appeared to meet Horikoshi's needs perfectly, but he was worried that it might not have been designed to fasten surface plate. Wouldn't it come out or be loosened by vibration? These questions caused some hesitation, but in the end the driving desire to reduce air resistance decided Horikoshi in favor of using the flush rivet.

Horikoshi's attempts to make the plane as light and slender as possible had to overcome a number of obstacles, one of which was the engine to be installed in the aircraft. Mitsubishi made its own engines, and naturally favored the one it had designated for the job. Horikoshi found it too heavy, however, to fit into the hull and still obtain the streamlining he desired. The company's engine manufacturers were not pleased with his alternative choice—the lighter Kotobuki (long life) engine made by rival Nakajima. In the end, however, he was allowed to have his way, and the Nakajima engine was installed in the new aircraft.

A second obstacle to speed and light weight was the choice of landing gear. At this time, retractable landing gear was the fashion in aircraft all over the world. The most important quality in a fighter, however, is maneuverability in air combat, and in the interest of that, Horikoshi had to rethink his position. In air combat, violent movement of the aircraft can create forces acting upon it of three to four times its weight. It was important, therefore, to reduce the plane's weight by as much as possible. For the sake of streamlining Horikoshi wanted to adopt retractable gear, but he found that such gear would increase the weight of the plane by forty to fifty kilograms. This was not an increase in weight that could be supported by the engine used in the aircraft and still obtain the required speed. Although the engine was of the 600-horsepower class, it was still 30 to 40 percent smaller than comparable engines being used in the world.

In the end, Horikoshi opted for a fixed-position landing gear of a single cantilever type. Its air resistance was lower than for ordinary fixed position gear by 30 percent, and it was estimated that in combination with the flushed rivets used on the aircraft's surfaces, the fixed landing gear would achieve almost the same reduction in air resistance as retractable gear.

In January 1935, just ten months after the start of design, the first prototype of the Ninth Development Project single-seat fighter was ready for flight testing. The outline of the fuselage was full of sharp beauty, in contrast to that of the plane created for the Seventh Development Project. The fuselage and wings gleamed with new paint—also covering up flush rivets of bad workmanship and uneven joins in the plating.

At the same time, the Nakajima company's prototype was also reported to be ready. The design was also a low mono-wing, but fabric-covered and with bracing wires and fixed-position landing gear of the same configuration as the P-26 fighter plane made by the Boeing company and just adopted by the U.S. Army. It was said to have easily exceeded 400 kilometers per hour in the company's tests.

Mitsubishi's own test flights began on February 3 at the Kagamigahara Airfield. Once again, company pilot Kajima took the controls.

The results, reported right away to the Naval Aeronautical Establishment, were believed only with difficulty and at once the Establishment decided to confirm the speeds obtained for itself, using Lieutenant Commander Yoshito Kobayashi of the flight testing section at Kagamigahara Airfield.

On the day Kobayashi flew the plane, Horikoshi and others came to watch. They watched as Kobayashi exceeded even the company's maximum expectation of the aircraft's speed. Suspicious, Kobayashi decided to check the accuracy of the speedometer. He placed two pieces of cloth on the ground at an interval of 2,000 meters. Then he flew back and forth between them, keeping for the sake of accurate calibration to the dangerously low altitude of twenty meters. Not convinced even by that, he repeated the test run using a stopwatch in the plane. That satisfied him, and in a final speed test, achieved 450 kilometers per hour at an altitude of 3,200 meters.

It was a remarkable result. The world's newest plane at that time had reached only 410 kilometers per hour. Not only that, but the speed of the carrier-borne fighter about to be adopted, the Type 95 made by Nakajima, was 350 kilometers per hour. Horikoshi and his team had designed a plane that flew faster than any other military plane in the world, and had achieved a jump in the increase in the speed of Japanese fighters, annually progressing up till then at from ten to twenty kilometers per hour, of 100 kilometers per hour. The engineers went mad with joy.

These great achievements in speed did not put off a major problem with the aircraft, however. Because it was so light, the plane could not sink fast enough in landing. Pinpoint landings were therefore very difficult to make. This defect, not remediable in the number one prototype (destroyed after strength tests) was fixed completely in the second one by adopting a recent American invention, the split flap.

With the number two prototype of its single-seat fighter Mitsubishi amazed official reviewers even more. At its official test flight before naval officers, it demonstrated a speed of zoom and deep dive never seen before. Officers steeped in the perception that Japanese aeronautics were well behind the rest of world had to rub their eyes at what they were seeing. With one aircraft, Japan had leapt ahead of everyone else. Pride and surprise at this achievement was almost overwhelming. After watching the second prototype's tests, Vice Admiral Kenji Maehara, the director of the Aeronautical Establishment, summed up the general reaction in a voice almost choked with emotion: "I have never been impressed as much as I am today. I am filled with only joy, knowing that such a plane has appeared in Japan at last. It is as if I am looking at a foreign plane of supreme excellence."

Fighter pilots were equally amazed at the fighter's performance. In their eyes, the aircraft's most critical characteristic was its dogfighting quality. The Japanese held that maneuverability was the deciding factor in dogfighting, and in this department, the biplane had long proved itself. But even here, the new mono-wing outdid the navy's newest fighter, the Type 95 biplane.

The new fighter was not the only outstanding success for Mitsubishi in 1935. The firm had also been working on a new land-based torpedo bomber (later designated Type 96, code name: Nell). It had been developed by another team in Horikoshi's department headed by Suero Honjo, who had suggested to Horikoshi the use of flush rivets. This aircraft also performed beyond world standards, and Mitsubishi went on to produce 636 of them.

With a change of engine, modifications to the airframe and the addition of carrier landing gear, the Horikoshi's new single-seat fighter was adopted by navy as the Type 96 carrier-borne fighter (code name: Claude). The designation 96, also given to the land-based torpedo bomber, was in honor of the year Kigen, 2,596 years after the legendary founding of the Japanese nation.

About 1,000 Type 96 fighters were made, 782 at the Nagoya Aircraft Works and the remainder at the Sasebo Naval Yard and the works of the Kyushu Airplane Company.

With these two planes, Japan had at last broken free of its dependence on foreign aircraft design. Of even greater significance, was that this independence had been achieved with great originality and style. Both the planes were excellent performers, beyond the country's and the world's expectations. Compared to Great Britain's Hawker Nimrod, France's Dewoitane D 510, Germany's Heinkel He-112, and

America's P2PA, the Type 96 fighter was far ahead. Its design established the direction of development for small and medium-size fighter aircraft in the years to come. The biplane had lost supremacy once and for all.

Flushed with the success of the Type 96 aircraft, Japanese aircraft designers now confidently pursued aircraft design alone. The purchase of foreign aircraft for other than comparison purposes ceased.

Three

The year 1937 (Showa 12—the twelfth year of the Showa Emperor Hirohito's reign) began, and on April 6 of that year an airplane called the Kamikaze (divine wind) belonging to the Asahi Newspaper Company departed Tokyo's Tachikawa Airfield. Its destination was London. Piloting the flight was Masaaki Iinuma. Kenji Tsukagoshi was engineer.

The flight was the object of a contest in a campaign to raise public interest in Japanese aviation. The Asahi Newspaper Company offered a prize to the reader who could guess what was expected to be a record flying time to London. The flight was more than a publicity stunt, however. Though civil-registered, the aircraft was the number two prototype of the army's high-speed Type 97 reconnaissance plane (code name: Babs). The idea for the aircraft had been suggested by Lieutenant Commander Yuzo Fujita, and engineer Naruo Ando of the Technical Research Center of the army. Mitsubishi's Nagoya Aircraft Works completed the project with engineer Fumihiko Kono, as chief designer and Shokichi Mizuno, Tomio Kubo, and others assisting.

The Type 97 reconnaissance plane was equipped with the Nakajima Aircraft Company's HA-8 type engine of 550 horsepower (maximum output was 740 horsepower at an altitude of 4,300 meters). Before the show flight to London, the aircraft had already reached 480 kilometers per hour in test flight. On the Tokyo–London flight, it covered the 15,357 kilometers in ninety-four hours, seventeen minutes and fifty-six seconds, establishing a new world record.

This was bright news against a darkening backdrop of international and domestic tensions. On January 15, 1936, Japan had withdrawn from the disarmament conference. Germany and Italy began to become aggressive in Europe; Italy invaded Ethiopia.

In Japan, politics took a direct turn toward militarism with the assassination by young army officers of two former premiers, Minoru Saito and Korekiyo Takahashi, Jotaro Watanabe, the inspector general of military training, on the night of February 26, 1936. The 2-26 incident, as it is known in Japan, resulted in the country openly drawing closer to the Fascist powers of Europe. By the end of the year, Japan had signed the Anti-Comintern Pact with Germany and Italy. Relations with Great Britain and the United States reached a new low.

It was in this heated atmosphere that Joji Hattori, manager of the design section of the technical division at Nagoya Aircraft Works, was summoned in May 1937, to meet Naota Goto, director of the works. When Hattori entered the office, Goto took from his desk a document with the navy's top secret stamp upon it. He handed it to Hattori.

"Just arrived from the head office," he said. "It's the proposal for this year's [12Si (Showa 12)] development plan for the carrier-borne fighter from Aeronautical Headquarters."

Hattori stayed on his feet as he took the document. He began to read the list of specifications.

- Maximum speed: more than 500 kilometers per hour at an altitude of 4,000 meters.
- Climb Rate: less than three minutes thirty seconds to 3,000 meters.
- Endurance: from 1.2 to 1.5 hours at nominal horsepower in regular condition at an altitude of 3,000 meters.
- Dogfighting performance: Not inferior to the Type 96 carrier-borne fighter, Model 2, Mode 1.
- Armament: two sets of 20-millimeter cannons. Two sets of 7.7-millimeter machine guns.

As Hattori took the figures in, Goto saw the designer's face harden and his body become still with tension. The man was still gazing intensely at the paper as Goto spoke again.

"These are startling requirements, aren't they?" he said. "Details will be shown officially in due course. The development seems to be a competition between our company and Nakajima Aircraft Company again. Head office is telling us to accept it at any risk."

Hattori nodded. Goto watched him anxiously. To both men these latest requirements were a shock after the success of the Type 96 carrier-borne fighter. That aircraft had already set a whole new standard and had been difficult enough to create, besides. After that, the new requirements seemed excessive. Goto and Hattori knew, however, that there could be no arguing with requirements received from the navy or army. Though the proposal Hattori had in his hand was a preliminary one, it was virtually a command.

Hattori took the proposal back to the offices of the design section. There he pondered an approach to the project. Unconsciously his eyes settled on Jiro Horikoshi, who had designed both the 7Si and Type 96 carrier-borne fighters. He was the only man, Hattori knew, who could head up such a demanding project. He called Horikoshi into his office. Without a word he handed him the navy's proposal. Horikoshi went back to his desk and opened it.

As he read the figures, Horikoshi felt that someone must be dreaming. It had been extremely difficult to develop the Type 96 fighter. That, he felt, was the limit of his capacities as a designer. To demand the performance specifications he was reading now was beyond him, and not necessary, either. Judging by other fighters imported to make comparisons, the Type 96 fighter was already among the world's finest. And if you took into account that it achieved its great performance using a 600-horsepower engine that was smaller than the power plants of other fighters, the Type 96 was the best. Further, its capabilities were not even known to the world yet. It was still a well-kept secret.

The more Horikoshi considered the 12Si specifications, the more impossible they seemed to him from a design standpoint. For example, the maximum speed recorded by the Type 96's prototypes was 450 kilometers per hour at 3,200 meters. But here they were demanding 500 kilometers per hour at 4,000 meters. It would not be easy to make a fighter to satisfy that requirement. And if Horikoshi did satisfy it, then other requirements suffered. A plane was a balance of requirements. Emphasizing one was at the expense of another. With the specifications he had before him, that balance would be next to impossible to achieve. For example, greater speed would decrease maneuverability, a major factor in dogfighting performance. Yet the new plane's dogfighting ability was supposed to be equal at least to the slower Type 96. Then there were the armament specifications. The Type 96 already carried two sets of 7.7-millimeter machine guns. Adding twin sets of the heavier 20-millimeter cannon would increase air resistance. That in turn would decrease speed and the climb rate and add other inhibitions to the dogfighting performance.

The greatest obstacle to the project revolved around the aircraft's power plant. To achieve the navy's new requirements a much more powerful engine would be needed. The Japanese aircraft industry, however, did not make such an engine. Their engines were smaller. There were good reasons for using small-size engines in carrier-borne fighters. But when it came to these new requirements the navy appeared to be ignoring reality.

On the other hand, there were very strong pressures to develop a new plane. Horikoshi estimated that it would take about three years to bring a new fighter through design and testing stages to production. Meanwhile, around the world aircraft development was proceeding at a dazzling rate and in those three years he could expect many excellent new planes to emerge from other countries. While Japan had an excellent fighter now, if development ceased with the Type 96, sooner or later the country would fall behind progress elsewhere.

That could have very serious consequences. Naturally, the navy had to have a fighter able to match those of any enemy, considered on a country by country basis. For the navy, however, the most formidable enemy was the United States. America not only designed and built excellent aircraft, the country's rich natural resources and well-developed industrial complex ensured self-sufficient production on a massive scale. Japan, on the other hand, had to import most materials for aircraft production. In this situation, in the event of war, only a decisive out matching of the enemy's aircraft would produce a strong advantage for Japan. That would require a fighter of drastically higher performance than any made now.

Horikoshi had no confidence that he could build such a plane. But he felt he had no choice. A designer's job was to build new things, and if the navy's requirements were next to impossible, well, their requirements for the design of the Type 96 fighter hadn't looked very possible either. Still, Horikoshi was full of doubt, and as he sat at his desk, his eyes stared absent-mindedly at the windowpane shining in his room in the sun of early summer.

At the time of seeing the preliminary proposals for the 12Si fighter, Horikoshi was deeply engaged in Mitsubishi's crash effort to design the 11Si carrier-borne bomber. The development of this aircraft had originally been a competition between the Nakajima Aircraft and Aichi Airplane companies, but at the last minute Mitsubishi had jumped into the race too. The lateness of the company's entry gave its designers only three months (till August 1937), to complete their fundamental plan for the bomber. In these circumstances, Horikoshi had little time to consider the 12Si fighter. Still, he made arrangements for engineer Ryuichiro Matsufuji, in charge of wind tunnel tests at Nagoya, to make a study of a wing section for the new plane. Matsufuji ran a first wind tunnel test on June 5, just days after Horikoshi had seen the preliminary 12Si proposals.

Then, on July 7, 1937, the international situation suddenly heated up. On that day, Chinese and Japanese troops at the Lukouchiao Bridge in a suburb of Peking exchanged gunfire. Though Japan immediately declared a policy of non-expansion, Japanese troops in North China launched a full-scale attack. A month later, they seized Peking.

Newspaper photos of the occupation of Peking created great excitement throughout Japan. It was in that atmosphere that the Nagoya Aircraft Works received an urgent letter from the Aeronautical Headquarters of the navy. The letter stated that the preliminary 12Si fighter requirements given to Mitsubishi in May two months before would now be explained in detail to the heads of the companies' design teams. At Mitsubishi, Horikoshi had already been appointed to that position. Joji Hattori sent him down alone to the briefing.

At the Yokosuka Base of the Naval Air Corps, where the Aeronautical Establishment was located, Horikoshi met with Lieutenant Commander Goro Wada. Wada, chief of staff of the fighter section of Aeronautical Headquarters, explained that the war between China and Japan was spreading. This was the reason behind the navy's urgent need for a new fighter.

Horikoshi knew that the requirements were meant to be followed. Still, he hoped that since they were preliminary and not final, some room might exist for compromise. He replied to Wada therefore that the requirements given him were far too severe for such urgency.

Wada, however, offered him no choice. "Of course we understand that," he replied. "However, we must have the very best."

From Wada's tone, Horikoshi knew that any argument with the requirements, however demanding, was now fruitless because they represented a consensus among all concerned interests throughout the navy about what was needed in a new carrier-borne fighter. The process of forming requirements began at Naval Headquarters. There, strategic needs were first defined. Then the combined fleet had its say. The Aeronautical Establishment was then handed the requirements and in turn passed them on to its flight test squadron at Yokosuka and its operational corps. With their opinions added, the proposal and its requirements were at last ready. At that stage any objection would mean going against the entire navy. In any case, higher management in the aircraft companies would agree with the navy's requirements, for management had only to place the work on the shoulders of the engineers in their design departments.

Horikoshi returned to Nagoya and told Hattori that there was no chance of any change in the specifications and that an all-out effort on the project would be necessary. Hattori went to see the director of the works and had Horikoshi transferred from the 11Si bomber project.

No sooner had Horikoshi become fully committed to the 12Si carrier-borne fighter project than electrifying news arrived. On August 14, Chinese aircraft bombed the Shanghai Joint Settlement. The next day twenty Japanese bombers crossed the East China Sea from Omura Air Base, and attacked Shanghai and Nanking. A strike of such long range was rare at this time and it created a sensation. Nowhere, however, was there more excitement than at the Nagoya Aircraft Works, for the aircraft used in the strike were Type 96 land-based torpedo bombers, created by Suero Honjo of Nagoya's design section. This was good news for Horikoshi's design ideas.

As the strikes continued through the late summer and autumn, however, the bombers began to suffer disconcerting losses. A fighter escort wasn't available for them over such a long range, and the Chinese fighters proved fiercer and more numerous than expected. With no long-range fighter available, the navy decided to move its escorts closer to the front. The aircraft carrier *Kaga,* loaded with Type 96 fighters, was dispatched, while more Type 96 fighters took up station at the newly repaired Kungtai Air Base, in the suburbs of Shanghai.

This was the battle test of Horikoshi's fighter. The Chinese air force at the time consisted of foreign-made planes, the American-made Curtiss Hawk 75, the Soviet I-15 and I-16, and England's Glouster Gladiator. In early encounters, the Type 96 fighter quickly proved victorious. On December 2, 1937, however, the superiority of the Type 96 fighter over foreign makes was spectacularly demonstrated. On that day a squadron of Type 96 fighters led by Lieutenant Nango shot down ten Soviet-made I-16s over Nanking. After that, the Chinese air force stayed at home. Japanese pilot skill was credited with part of the victory, but there was no doubt that the qualities of the Type 96 had proved decisive.

Though this news and the success of the land-based torpedo bomber were very encouraging to Horikoshi the difficulties of the 12Si fighter project had not ceased to worry him deeply. In their August meeting, Lieutenant Commander Wada had already told Horikoshi there could be no change in the demanding requirements named in the preliminary proposal. But when, on October 5, Horikoshi was given the secret document containing the requirements in final form, he was dismayed by what he read, page by page. The final requirements were even more demanding than the preliminary ones.

- Purpose: Escort fighter with dogfighting performance superior to that of the enemy light weight fighters. Also, the aircraft must be able to act as an interceptor which can catch and destroy enemy attack planes.
- Maximum speed: More than 500 kilometers per hour (270 knots) at 4,000 meters.
- Climb rate: Less than three minutes, thirty seconds to 3,000 meters.
- Endurance: In regular conditions: from 1.2 hours to 1.5 hours at nominal horsepower at 3,000 meters.
- In overloaded conditions: from 1.5 to 2.0 hours at nominal horsepower, more than six hours at cruising speed, at an altitude of 3,000 meters.

- Runway length to take off: Less than 70 meters with a headwind of 12 meters per second.
- Landing Speed: Less than 58 knots (107 kilometers per hour)
- Sinking Rate: At gliding; from 3.5 meters per second to 4.0 meters per second.
- Dogfight performance: Not to be inferior to the Type 96 carrier-borne fighter Model 2 Mode 1.
- Armaments: Two sets of 20-millimeter cannons. Two sets of 7.7-millimeter machine guns.
- Bomb load (overloaded condition):   Two sixty-kilogram bombs or two thirty-kilogram bombs.
- Wireless installations: One set of Type 96 Model Ku-1 radio; one set of Type Ku Model Ku-3 direction finder.
- Other equipment: Oxygen inhaler; fire extinguisher; night lights; standard meters.
- Strength: Case A (later phase of pulling up)—Load factor 7.0 with safety margin 1.8.
- Case B (earlier phase of pulling up)—Load factor 7.0 with safety margin 1.8.
- Case C (at the limited diving speed)—Load factor 2.0 with safety margin 1.8.
- Case D (pulling up from inverted flight)—Load factor 3.0 with safety margin 1.8.

Though he accepted his duty to create a new fighter to such radically high standards, Horikoshi had never been fully confident of success. Finding even more severe demands in the final requirements did little to dispel his sense of doubt. In particular he noted an increase in the range required of the fighter with the inclusion of the direction finder, now to have long-range capability in addition to other features that would be difficult enough to fulfill, such as greatly higher speed. He also worried about the wing mounting of the twenty-millimeter cannon. With this arrangement, only poor hit rates had been achieved in other countries, and it was still considered experimental. Now he had to make wing-mounted guns work. And he had to overcome the weight and resistance problems also inherent in the arrangement. Horikoshi's greatest concern, however, remained the same as when he had first looked at the project: To go as fast and as far and be as maneuverable as required, the 12Si fighter had to have a big engine, and Japan simply did not make such an engine.

Underlying all his worries was the lack of flexibility in such detailed requirements. This had been his protest all along. From a designer's point of view, an aircraft was a harmony of requirements, because in practice they tended to reduce one another. Establishing a harmony meant keeping all the requirements in balance, avoiding an emphasis on speed, for example, that might be gained at the excessive sacrifice of other requirements. Yet the final requirements he had now were rigidly spelled out. He had been given no room to move. Except in one area, and it wasn't much—no armor protection was required for the pilot or the fuel tanks in the wings.

In those days, armor on planes was still not considered important in many countries. The doctrine that offense was the best defense for fighters meant that speed and maneuverability in dogfighting took precedence in fighter design. The Japanese in particular had traditionally been wedded to this approach. Horikoshi had some objection to this, but with the stiffness of the other requirements to overcome already, he was glad merely of the saving of weight that it meant.

Faced with so little flexibility to deal with the high requirements, Horikoshi became even more deeply worried about how he was to succeed with the 12Si fighter. The only consolation appeared to be that if he could succeed, he would have made the very best fighter in the world. Meanwhile however, he became so obsessed with the problems that he fell ill. One night he suffered a severe pain in his chest. Doctors diagnosed a lung infection that had become a great infiltration—an ailment he had developed shortly after he had completed the Type 96 fighter. He was confined to his home.

A month passed before he could return to work. In that time Horikoshi was only driven closer to a demand for more leeway in dealing with the requirements for the 12Si project. He thought to himself that these requirements, however strict, were only requirements. His job as an engineer was to do his best with them as possible. If he didn't meet each exactly, he would still be justified if he achieved an improvement in performance and kept the fighting power of the aircraft to a maximum. Coming to this conclusion made him feel better. When Horikoshi returned to work, he thought he could glimpse at last a dim light at the end of the tunnel, but his hopes were quickly shot down.

At the beginning of the new year, on January 7, 1938, the navy and the aircraft companies held a meeting to study jointly the proposal for the 12Si fighter at the Aeronautical Establishment. Horikoshi went with Yoshitoshi Sone, Sadahiko Kato, and his section head, Joji Hattori.

On entering the conference room they were struck at once by the large number of important naval personnel attending. It was an indication of how extraordinary were their expectations for the new fighter. Besides Rear Admiral Kenji Maehara, director of the Aeronautical Establishment, there was also every division head. These included Rear Admiral Misao Wada, one of the pioneers of naval aviation in Japan and now director of the technical department, and Lieutenant Commander Takeo Shibata, the chief of staff of the fighter section. In addition they recognized Lieutenant Commander Minoru Genda, commander of the fighter group at Yokosuka Naval Air Corps. Genda's face was still sunburned after his recent return from duty in China. Finally, five engineers from the Nakajima Aircraft Company were also present. They were Mitsubishi's rivals in the 12Si competition.

Kenji Maehara and Misao Wada opened the meeting with the statement that the war in China would not end soon. International tensions were increasing. For these reasons, the air forces needed strengthening. The 12Si carrier-borne fighter was very important to this aim. They then went over the requirements for the plane, and a lively discussion followed.

Lieutenant Commander Genda's views were of particular interest. Genda had just returned from central China, where he had been an aviation staff officer in the Second Joint Naval Air Corps. With direct experience of the air fighting in China, gained from directing operations with both the Type 96 and Type 95 fighters, he was emphatic that the dogfighting capability had to be greatly improved.

Genda's voice was only one among the chorus of naval officers at the meeting demanding new standards of performance. Some even suggested requirements beyond those that already had Horikoshi so worried.

The engineers from the companies said little in reply. The navy's demands were understandable, but technically far from reality. They weren't left just to listen, however. The opinion of the companies was asked, and it was Horikoshi who stood up. His face was pale after his illness, and with all his worrying, his expression stiff and distorted.

"Thank you for your valuable opinions." he began. "However, frankly speaking, all the items of the requirement plan are intended to create a plane superior to the fighters of any other country. Range, speed, climbing rate, payload, and maneuverability are all of the very highest standard. We can understand your intention behind these requirements, but it is most unreasonable to put all of these requirements in any one fighter. Each one of them—range, speed, climbing rate, and furthermore payload and maneuverability are mutually contradictory. To make them a reality simultaneously with engines of small power is extremely difficult from the technical viewpoint. I have heard opinions that the requirements for our attack and other kinds of planes would be satisfied if they were equal to the first-grade planes of other countries. The requirements for the 12Si carrier-borne fighter are too high in comparison with this approach. Isn't there any room for a little easing of the requirements?"

As Horikoshi finished, his audience, so full of high expectations for the new fighter, became tense. But after a violent exchange of opinions among themselves, the naval officers had only one answer for the engineers. "There is absolutely no room to ease the requirements."

The engineers quit the conference with a promise to spare no effort to build the plane. But both Hattori and Horikoshi were even gloomier about success than before. The navy's severity about the requirements at the conference had now completely removed any hope of flexibility. Furthermore, Mitsubishi had already accepted the project. That left the design section to beat its own way out of the bush.

This frustrating position was not improved by the news that the Nakajima company had decided to withdraw from the competition. No clear reasons were given, but Horikoshi and his fellow engineers could guess that it was because Nakajima's designers also saw little prospect of success with the inflexible application of such drastic requirements.

Hattori and Horikoshi got organized for the design work. The first step was to assign a design team. Yoshitoshi Sone, a graduate from Tokyo University's College of Engineering, was assigned to make the calculations. He was given two assistants, both graduates of the university's aeronautical school, Takeshi Nakamura, and Teruo Tojo. Yoshitoshi Sone also had charge of structure, along with four assistants, Yoshio Yoshikawa, Sadao Doi, Toshihiko Narahara, and Shokichi Tomita. The power plant design was given to Denichiro Inoue and Shotaro Tanaka. Armaments went to Fukuizumi Hatakenaka, Yoichi Ohashi, Hideo Koda, Shokichi Shibayama, and Miyoshi Eguchi. Sadahiko Kato, Takeyoshi Mori, and Keizo Nakao too were in charge of landing gear. Management of the group and was the responsibility of Kumataro Takenaka, who was also chief of the maintenance crew.

With the team ready, work on the fundamental design of the plane began in earnest. Horikoshi's basic aim was of course to reduce the weight and air resistance of the aircraft as much as possible, and especially since he would have to work with small engines. A light weight and low resistance were the only means by which a small engine could be made to meet the requirements.

The first design task was to select an engine. An aircraft was built around its engine. A big engine increased the size of a plane, but in the case of carrier-borne fighters there were already size limits. The plane had to be handled easily on the carrier's deck, and could not be too large. Above all, of course, bigness was not favored by fighter pilots. A small, light plane was the most maneuverable, and maneuverability was key in dogfighting.

Under these circumstances, Horikoshi had a choice of two types of air-cooled radial engines, the Zuisei (Star of Fortune) and Kinsei (Venus). Mitsubishi made both. Ideally, Horikoshi wanted something between these two. The Kinsei delivered 1,100 horsepower at 4,200 meters, the Zuisei 875 at 3,600 meters. However, he chose the smaller Zuisei, to reduce weight. Even so, it was estimated that the Zuisei would make the new fighter 50 percent heavier than the Type 96 fighter. However, installing the Kinsei would have produced a much greater increase, 70 to 80 percent. Horikoshi felt that this would be unacceptable to pilots.

Once the Zuisei engine had been selected, the form of the fuselage, the size of the wings and the weight of the airframe could be estimated. Several drawings were made on this basis and performance calculations carried out.

The design process proceeded rapidly. Wind tunnel tests of the main wing section were finished by February 17, just over a month after Horikoshi's depressing January 8 meeting with the top brass of the Aeronautical Establishment. In designing the wing section, engineer Ryuichiro Matsufuji, in charge of wind tunnel tests, studied the advantages of those used in the Type 96 carrier-borne fighter, the Type 96 land-based torpedo bomber, and the army's Type 97 reconnaissance plane. Matsufuji suggested a wing area that was boldly big in relation to the weight of the plane. It had the demerit of increasing the aircraft's weight and reducing speed. But Matsufuji advised that there was no other choice if the design group wanted to increase dogfighting and turning abilities and make the plane easy to take-off and land on an aircraft carrier.

In addition it was decided to make the wing area bigger and the fuselage longer in order to improve the accuracy of the twin sets of twenty-millimeter cannons mounted in the wings. The reasoning behind this was the same as that used in explaining the accuracy of a rifle over a pistol. A longer barrel was more steady. The strong recoil of the cannons would be modified by greater length and stability in the air. The wing span was to be no greater than twelve meters, however, so as to fit onto the elevators of the aircraft carriers.

As with the Type 96 fighter, Horikoshi's attempts to save weight produced original approaches. One was to use a one-piece instead of a two-piece wing. This eliminated the heavy metal fittings necessary to attach a two-piece wing to the fuselage. What fittings were required were made as small as possible. Another weight reduction technique was to hollow out portions of the aircraft not contributing to its strength. This process was called "meat trimming." Windows were cut out of duralumin plates, and holes bored in other places. The process was carried out so thoroughly that strength calculations had to be constantly checked to make certain the "meat trimming" didn't go too far.

While developing these weight-reducing measures, a constant search for new materials that could further keep weight down led to the discovery of an even stronger version of duralumin. E.S.D.T. was a super-ultra duralumin recently developed to practical standards by Dr. Isamu Igarashi and an engineer, Ozeki, of the Sumitomo Metal Company. It had a tensile strength 30 to 40 percent greater than ordinary super duralumin. It was very important to be able to use less metal since aircraft materials had to be imported. With permission from the Aeronautical Establishment, Horikoshi used E.S.D.T. to make the wing spars for his new fighter.

For the plane's landing gear, Horikoshi decided to adopt a re-tractable design, the first such use in a Japanese fighter. His basic intention was to contribute to low air resistance in a fighter that was larger than the Type 96. It was also, however, easier to use retractable gear with larger wings.

Horikoshi considered that there would not be time to design new landing gear. The navy was in too much of a hurry. Instead, he gave permission to engineer Sadahiko Kato, in charge of landing gear, to imitate another make. Kato chose the landing gear of the American Vought V-143, an example of which had been brought by the army.

On April 6, 1938, a first full-size wooden mockup of the 12Si fighter was ready. Only eleven months had passed since Hattori, the head of the design section at Nagoya, had handed Horikoshi the preliminary requirements for the fighter. Now it was a three-dimensional reality. The airframe was larger than the Type 96 fighter's, and very slender in shape. The parabolic shape of the wing tips was in harmony with the tail planes and constituted a beautiful unity of design. Even the arma-ments and communication equipment, installed as if ready for flight, seemed to fit in especially well with the design.

Nevertheless, as Horikoshi and his colleagues looked over the mockup, they had mixed feelings. The high requirements so inflexibly demanded by the navy had been beyond the standards of Japanese aeronautical technology at the time. In an effort to meet them, the designers had had to forgo convention and come up with original ap-proaches to the aircraft's design. They could take great satisfaction in that. They had worked, however, in the certainty that they would not be able to meet all the requirements. That simply wasn't possible, given the technology available and the inflexible attitude of the navy. Through the long, difficult days of development, an atmosphere of depression had often reigned. Only their pride at not being beaten by the engineers of other countries had kept them going. And now they were faced with the difficult process of constructing an actual flying model, using new materials, to prove their new design ideas.

As Horikoshi ran his fingers over the smooth wooden surfaces of the mockup, he could not rid himself of anxiety about what problems and objections he would encounter in the next stages of development. He and his team had worked to the very limit of their capacities as designers. But it could not be avoided—what was needed now to com-plete the design successfully was some flexibility in the requirements.

Otherwise it would never be possible to harmonize the design fully. The navy would now have to inspect the mock-up. Horikoshi intended to bring up the flexibility question once again during this process.

The inspection process for the mock-up began with a meeting at which Horikoshi gave officers of the Aeronautical Establishment a pre-inspection briefing on the mockup's design. This was an important occasion, attended by Horikoshi, four members of his team, and about thirty officers from the Establishment, including Lieutenant Commander Takeo Shibata, head of the fighter section, and the Establishment's second in command, Lieutenant Commander Minoru Genda, the fighter group commander.

Horikoshi began the meeting with a detailed description and developmental history of each feature of the mock-up's design. His talk followed a schedule titled "The Description of the Plan of the A6M1" (code name of the 12Si, or Zero Fighter) submitted to the navy three days before.

As he spoke, Horikoshi had to answer many questions. When there were no more, he got to his feet and said, "I have a question. As it is written in the submitted A6M1 plan, it is very difficult to meet all the plan requirements from the technical viewpoint. Meeting these requirements is, of course, the responsibility of us aeronautical engineers. However, an airplane cannot be made only from the design techniques of engineers. The materials and all others things which constitute the airplane come from other industries. In other words, it can be said that the production of an airplane depends on the technical standard of Japanese industries and their productive capacity. Fortunately, we were able to make use of super-ultra duralumin, the result of excellent development work at the Sumitomo Metal Company, but that does not mean that the industrial capacity of Japan needed to maintain this plane exceeds that of the leading Western countries. On the contrary, it cannot be doubted that we are far behind in certain divisions. With such small support from our industries, frankly speaking, it is very difficult to make the 12Si carrier-borne fighter meet the planned requirements. I say this because I want to make the plane as close to the requirements as possible. If we try to make the performances evenly close to the requirements, then by our calculation the maximum speed of the plane will be smaller than the requirement by ten knots and the dogfighting performance will be inferior to that of the Type 96 fighter specified in the requirements. Therefore, I would

like to ask you, under those unavoidable restrictions, how do you rate
the importance of range, speed, and dogfight performance? Since it is
impossible to satisfy all of them, I hope one of these requirements
can be reduced. So I beg you for the order of the importance."

Horikoshi sat down.

The naval officers sat in silence. Horikoshi had designed the Type
96 fighter, the pride of the navy. He was highly valued and not to be
taken lightly. Still, they were not pleased to be forced to consider an
answer.

They began to exchange opinions. As the discussion heated up,
however, it quickly turned into an argument between the two most
insistent—Lieutenant Commander Minoru Genda and Shibata, head
of the fighter section.

Genda mentioned some real cases of air fighting in China and
stated in a sharp voice: "After all, the fighter has a duty to dogfight
with enemy fighters and shoot them down. In other words, the value
of the fighter depends on whether it can win a dogfight or not.
Mitsubishi should of course satisfy the requirement plan for the 12Si
fighter, but if I were to dare to answer the question of engineer
Horikoshi, the dogfighting performance should come first in this new
fighter, too, and it absolutely should not be inferior to the Type 96
carrier-borne fighter. And to satisfy that dogfighting requirement, I
think the speed or the range can be sacrificed to some degree."

The Yokosuka-based Naval Air Corps to which Genda belonged
was in charge of the operational tests of newly developed planes. From
their up-to-date studies of air combat, the corps had come to the opinion that a fighter without good dogfighting ability was useless, and
since the spectacular victories of the Type 96 fighter in China this
view had become an article of faith. Those corps members attending
the conference with Genda of course supported his view completely.

Genda, however, faced the criticism of Lieutenant Commander
Shibata, head of the fighter section at the Aeronautical Establishment. Shibata also had wartime experience of air operations in China
as the fighter group commander on board the carrier *Kaga*. He had
been one of those expected to develop the 12Si carrier-borne fighter.

"I think the opinion of Lieutenant Commander Genda is very
reasonable," he began. "Certainly Japanese fighters are much superior in dogfighting performance, as was shown clearly by the results
of air battles with American and Soviet fighters. However, I don't

think a fighter's duties consist of dogfighting alone. We should re-
member that losses among the Type 96 land-based torpedo bomber,
which carried out the trans-ocean bombing raids, were unexpectedly
large. This means that even the excellent Type 96 torpedo bomber
absolutely needs the escort of a fighter, in spite of its high speed and
heavy defensive armament. As long as the escort of a bomber is one
of the duties of a fighter, then naturally the fighter is required to have
enough range to follow the bomber over long distances. Also, it was
shown clearly in air combat in China that the I-16 is slightly superior
to the Type 96 carrier-borne fighter in speed. Therefore, the I-16 could
often escape. To catch up with enemy fighters, a high speed is required.
There is a tendency in Japan to give dogfighting first importance, but
by opening our eyes wide to trends in future fighters, I believe we
should esteem range and speed as most important."

Shibata's counterargument only increased tension in the room and
he was soon the object of fierce rebuttals from Genda's supporters.
The flight test division of the Aeronautical Establishment to which
Shibata belonged naturally tended to be theoretical in its approach.
On the other hand, the Yokosuka Naval Air Corps did practical flight
testing and placed a high premium on war experience and training.
These differences soon made it apparent that there could be no end
to the debate.

In the face of this dispute, Horikoshi and his three colleagues
clammed up. They were appalled at what they were seeing. Having
asked for only a little flexibility in the requirements, they now realized that the navy could not make up its mind. The requirements they
had been trying to satisfy represented not only the necessities of fighter
design. They now saw they also represented the arguments about those
necessities.

When the meeting ended with no conclusion reached, the engineers left in a grim mood. It was plainly being left up to them to settle
the arguments by meeting all the requirements, just as they had been
originally given them. Once more, they had no room to move, while
having to accept responsibility for every decision made. With shoulders down they walked in silence along the road, already covered in
the darkness of evening.

Four

On April 27 of 1938, Lieutenant Eiichi Iwaya of the technical department of the Aeronautical Headquarters, Captain Kira, director of the flight test division of the Aeronautical Establishment, Lieutenant Shigeru Itaya of the Yokosuka Naval Air Corps, and many other officials concerned with fighters entered through the gate of the Nagoya Aircraft Works in a long string of cars. They were greeted by Director Goto, and after a short rest they entered the development factory of the first manufacturing division.

Inside, the full-sized mockup of the 12Si carrier-borne fighter waited for them, its smooth wooden surfaces shining quietly. The men gazed at the model without words. From the plan already submitted by Mitsubishi Heavy Industries and the plan explanation committee that had met two weeks previously they knew about the content of the aircraft's principal items. Still, a new, deep emotion caught them as they stood looking at the full-sized model.

Low mutters came from them. "Rather big, after all."

At that, the eyes of Horikoshi and others from the Nagoya works betrayed their anxiety. They remembered: "The fighter's main duty is dogfighting. So the first priority is maneuverability." The fighter pilots had insisted that counted most and for this reason, they had wanted a plane as small and light as possible. But the mockup of the 12Si carrier-borne fighter before them was quite different from their concept.

Whether the plane would be adopted or not by the navy depended on the opinions of the naval aeronautical officials gathered in the hangar. To gain their favor the design should have been of a light, small fighter. But Horikoshi had had no choice but to enlarge the plane to accommodate an engine that was required to be small, but was still nearly 50 percent greater in horsepower than the engine for the pilots' much-loved Type 96 carrier-borne fighter.

"Now start the first examination of the mockup of the 12Si carrier-borne fighter." So the officials openly invited the examiners to begin.

They crowded round the mockup. Actual-size models or real pieces of the aircraft's equipment were all in place in the airframe. The right and left wings housed twenty-millimeter cannons, and 7.7-millimeter machine guns were decked in front of the cockpit.

The officials inspected every part, comparing it with the description of the plan. Horikoshi's design team was subjected to sharp questions. Navy inspectors got into the cockpit and checked the visibility and the arrangement of the equipment. Others discussed the position of the foot steps by which to climb up into the cockpit.

Opinions that considered the views of the pilot and the ground crew who would actually operate and maintain the plane followed successively. The officials wrote instructions for modifications on the many blackboards that had been brought in. With uneasy faces, the designers jotted them down. At last, when the number of modifications had reached close to 100, the examination stopped.

The result of the mockup examination was fine for the most part. No fundamental modification was required. The faces of Horikoshi and his designers showed deep relief.

"Make the modifications required and continue the design." With that announcement, the examination of the first mockup ended.

At this time, the navy decided to adopt unofficially for this aircraft the constant-speed propeller made by the Sumitomo Metal Company through a production license purchased from the Hamilton Propeller Company of the United States.

The fixed-pitch propeller or the two-step variable-pitch propeller were commonly used for the airplanes of those days. However, these propellers had the disadvantage that the engine could not keep a regular rotation as the plane changed its speed, and the engine therefore could not give its maximum power.

This was a great disadvantage for a fighter that must change its speed quickly during air combat. In comparison with this, the constant-speed propeller quickly adjusted the pitch of the blades, automatically responding to the change of speed so the engine could keep its normal rotation. This type of propeller had never actually been used in Japan for an airplane. It was thought necessary for the 12Si fighter presently under development, however, because of the severe performance requirements.

It was also decided for the first time in the world to equip the fighter with a streamlined drop tank, to meet the requirement for a long range. The drop tank had been used by the Curtiss Hawk III and other aircraft before, but the range with these tanks was far below that planned for the Zero. The drop tank was installed on the underside of the fuselage. The gasoline within the tank was consumed on the inward journey to the destination. At sight of an enemy plane, it was dropped to lighten the fighter in preparation for combat. There were two traditional designs of these tanks: half moon and torpedo-shaped, each attachable to the bomb rack. As both were extremely big and air-resistant, Horikoshi worked to decrease their air resistance.

While the design was making such progress, the second mockup examination was held on July 11, 1938, by Lieutenant Commander Shibata of the Aeronautical Establishment, Lieutenant Commander Genda of the Yokosuka Naval Air Corps, and others. They confirmed that the modifications required of the first mockup had been carried out. The examination was completed without trouble. With that, the drawings began to flow to the development factory and the inspection section.

Security at the Nagoya Aircraft Works was most stringent at the development factory. The factory was a huge, closed room in which the final, approved mockup designs were turned into a working prototype by the design team. The army and navy officials stationed at the Nagoya works paid particularly strict attention to the development factory. It was also the main concern of the security department's guards.

Normal security arrangements at the Nagoya works were strict as it was. Incoming and outgoing personnel of the works were checked at the gates by the guard. For anyone to go in or out, permission of the guards was required. Anyone leaving was subjected to a body inspection. All employees were identified by badges, different for the management and workers.

Security for the development factory was even stricter. Only employees concerned and wearing a special badge were permitted to enter the area. Other people were prohibited from even looking inside the factory. Common employees did not even approach the area, fearing accidental suspicion.

As parts were produced from the drawings and inspected, they were taken to the development factory. The prototype was assembled inside the surround of a screen so no one could see from outside. The partial strength and function tests were carried out in parallel.

A hot summer began.

The drawings of the 12Si land-based torpedo bomber, the design of which had been developed in the same design section, began to flow into the development factory. Manufacturing was started secretly.

The design team for the twin-engine torpedo bomber was led by Suero Honjo and included engineers Nobuhiko Kusakabe, Shiro Kushibe, Hiroshi Oda, Isao Imai, and others. This team too had been struggling with severe requirements exceeding those normally expected for a twin-engine plane. Later, Sadahiko Kato, Denichiro Inoue, Tetsuro Hikita, and others joined this design team.

The members of Horikoshi's fighter design group knew that this land-based attack plane had many novel characteristics. The torpedo bomber's plans were based on lessons obtained from the battle experience of the Type 96 land-based torpedo bomber in the Japan-China fighting. The new torpedo bomber had to satisfy requirements of a high standard—in scout-load condition a range of 2,600 nautical miles (4,815 kilometers); overloaded for attack, with an 800-kilogram payload of bombs or a torpedo, it had to have a range of 2,000 nautical miles (3,700 kilometers). In addition, the plane had to have a high battle speed. To help meet these requirements, part of the structure of each wing was made into a fuel tank (an integral tank). Integral tanks were common in civilian aircraft, but were a drastic design innovation in military aircraft. Together, the bomber's wing tanks carried 5,000 liters of fuel.

A twenty-millimeter cannon was fitted in the tail and the body was shaped like a cigar so that gunners and other air crew members could pass through it. To prevent a decrease in performance, the bomber was like Horikoshi's new fighter, without any armor protection for the fuel tanks and the seats of the crew. At that time, American bombers already had protection against bullets in these areas. They considered it natural that a slow bomber should need protection against fast, agile fighters. The integral tanks of Honjo's new torpedo bomber could not have protection, however. To protect fuel tanks, as was done in American bombers, the integral tanks would have had to be given up. Without them, the plane would not have the fuel for the required range. Heated discussion within the navy and between the navy and the company arose about this problem. But in the end, the requirements triumphed. The unprotected integral tanks stayed.

Horikoshi often went to the Aeronautical Establishment and Aeronautical Headquarters. There he noticed a strange atmosphere developing in the navy. It did not take a clear form, but he began to suspect that some people in the navy did not have high expectations of the new fighter he was developing. Horikoshi thought it might be that because he had so often criticized the severity of the requirements, many officials had come to doubt that the aircraft's performance would realize the requirements.

This atmosphere instantly affected the engineers, including Horikoshi. Their calculations indicated that a plane close to the requirements could be accomplished, but concrete data based on actual performance could not be obtained until a prototype was completed. Horikoshi's suspicions shook his self-confidence slightly. Then they began coming into the open through a difference of interpretation between the navy and Horikoshi.

Horikoshi secretly learned that the navy had been asking Mitsubishi some questions about his new fighter. The questions made Horikoshi suspect that the navy was thinking of changing the fighter to an interceptor.

The new fighter he was developing combined both penetrator and interceptor characteristics. If it were changed to an interceptor, the range needed for a role as penetrator would naturally take a low priority. But if even that one range requirement was changed, the whole plane would have to be redesigned. For the fighter was a balance of characteristics designed to meet the particular requirements for its high performance.

On August 8, 1938, less than a month after the second mock-up of the Zero had been approved and the first prototype begun, Horikoshi went alone to the Aeronautical Headquarters. There he was informed that an exchange of opinions with Mitsubishi regarding the matter of the interceptor was indeed going on.

His suspicions then, were real. Horikoshi felt his mood sink. He asked if the fighter project under his direction was going to be changed.

The staffer smiled. "I am not saying such a thing. The response of Mitsubishi to the question is out of focus. Nobody mentioned changing the present plan of the fighter under development to an interceptor. Why do you misunderstand?"

"I understand very well," Horikoshi replied. But then he decided to be frank and complain. "However, successive questions of this kind may ruin the morale of subordinates."

"That is strange. It is natural for us to ask questions and you need not worry about it. Mitsubishi's worries are its own illusion," the staffer teased. "Everybody is very anxious for the completion of the plane under development. The navy is worried about nothing. If there is any worry, then it is on Mitsubishi's side. In other words, the performance of Mitsubishi's fighter caused the Zuisei type engine to be installed in the fighter under development." As the man said this, his face bore a stiff expression. Horikoshi knew what that meant.

An engine called the Sakae 12 had been completed by the Nakajima Aircraft Company. The Sakae 12 was only 3.2 centimeters bigger in diameter and four kilograms heavier in dry weight than the Zuisei engine made by Mitsubishi. Yet it developed 950 horsepower at 4,200 meters, against the Zuisei's 875 horsepower at an altitude of 3,600 meters. For the Type 96 carrier-borne fighter, Horikoshi had had to choose, unwillingly, Nakajima's Kotobuki Type 5 engine. The staffer was now hinting that Mitsubishi might again have to adopt an engine by rival company Nakajima for its new fighter. That would be unbearable.

The staffer went on: "For the first and second prototype, the engine can be the Zuisei because of the circumstances, but we want the third and fourth planes to be equipped as we recommend with the Sakae engine of the Nakajima Aircraft Company. To make a superb fighter, just listen to us and adopt the Sakae 12 engine. Then Mitsubishi will be said to be fair, and that's to your advantage, after all." He gazed at Horikoshi.

As a designer, of course, Horikoshi had no objection to the change of engine. He could not afford to care about saving the face of the company if it meant getting the plane close to the requirements. He had no choice but to take advantage of whatever would be useful to that goal.

"Anyway," the staffer continued, "we have the greatest expectations of the new fighter. We hope you'll make your best efforts to complete the plane."

Horikoshi nodded at these remarks. They made him feel light at heart, knowing that the navy had zeal for his new fighter. But the staffer was not finished.

"It is still under investigation, but it has been proposed to abolish the twenty-millimeter cannons and equip the aircraft with extra fuel tanks instead. Mitsubishi may have to do its own arrangements, so it has not been decided on what number of planes the change will be made. But when some of the planes are completed and production comes to a lull, please make drawings of the wing, wing fuel tanks, and fuel lines, and be prepared to make the change at any time."

"You mean to abolish the twenty-millimeter cannons?"

"Yes. We will give you instructions in due course. The argument for the abolition of the twenty-millimeter cannons is coming out from fighter corps. It is not yet at the stage for us to go into details, however, the abolition must be taken into account and you should proceed with preparations for that." The staff member said that much, then went silent.

Horikoshi was caught by a violent rush of feeling. Although his fear that the fighter would be changed to an interceptor had been lessened by the staffer's remarks, the argument for abolishing the twenty-millimeter cannons looked to have an unlikable persistence about it.

The twenty-millimeter cannons planned for the Zero were two sets of the Type 99 Model 1, Mark 3 of a fixed type made by Dai Nihon Weapons. The combined weight of the two sets was 46.4 kilograms, but it became a lot more when the weight of the structure needed to support the cannons, and two magazines of sixty bullets each were included. These weights were in the calculation of the design. The abolition of the cannons would force quite a lot of design change. The proposal for the cannons' abolition created a strong anxiety in Horikoshi, who had so prudently built up the Zero's design.

He visited the head office of the company with a discouraged expression on his face and reported the points to the section chief, Yashima. Then he returned to Nagoya.

Over the late summer, the source of the twenty-millimeter cannons' abolition proposal gradually began to be known to him. He began to suspect that it was the opinions of the air corps in the field that were causing such a disturbance among the navy's officials at Aeronautical Headquarters. But it was not until the fall that Horikoshi at last learned the reasons for the change.

One day he was called to the director's office. "Such a thing from the Aeronautical Headquarters," Director Goto said. His face was dark. Horikoshi took the document.

Beside the letterhead "Twelfth Air Corps Confidential No. 169" was written "Opinions regarding the performance required of the fighter under development, based on battle experiences in the present incident."

It was the written opinion of the Twelfth Air Corps in China. The corps had been engaged mainly in fighter battles. The corps was obviously expressing dissatisfaction with the 12Si carrier-borne fighter under development by Horikoshi. The opinion began:

> In the battle experience of fighter squadrons escorting bombers on air raids on Hankow or Nanchang after the fall of Nanking, it is without question that dogfighting ability comes first among the performances of an escort fighter. It should be understood that it was mainly because of the inferior skill and poor fighting spirit of their pilots that the Chinese side was always defeated in spite of the fact that the number and performance of their planes were not lower than ours.
>
> Against enemies which have skill equal to us, it is hopeless without superior dogfighting ability to escort bombers over a long range and achieve our present purpose.
>
> There are not a few cases of air raids against enemy planes of excellent skill that took a long time to shoot down or lose because of a shortage of fuel. There were also hard fights surrounded by enemy planes superior in number and position. In such cases, we will fall an easy prey to opponents if dogfighting performance is inferior. Thus the escort fighter is required to be not inferior to any fighter of the world in dogfighting performance. It should be strictly forbidden to sacrifice the dogfighting performance so as to increase range.

The paper was stating that dogfight performance came first for the single-seat fighter, and if absolutely necessary, range could be sacrificed to this. It was also stating that in place of escort fighters on a long-distance air raid, the bombers should fly in a defensive formation. Like a hedgehog, the formation would bristle with machine guns. Of course, the extra machine guns would be carried at the expense of bomb payload. The paper was also pointing out the necessity of a land-based target defense fighter (an interceptor) that would have to be equipped with numerous machine guns at the expense of bomb payload. And finally, the paper was insisting on the need for a land-based defense fighter, for which climbing ability and speed were to be the first priority.

The air corps admitted the necessity for machine guns of an aperture of ten millimeters or thirteen millimeters, but opposed the twenty-millimeter cannon. The gun's muzzle velocity was too low, and in a strong tone, the air corps gave 100 demerit points without a single one for merit.

Horikoshi's face bore an anxious expression as he finished reading. "Does this mean decisively a change of plan?"

"No," replied Goto. "This paper is for information only, they said when this was handed over. However, the Twelfth Air Corps is a powerful corps in the war service. The navy may not be able to disregard such a strong opinion from the battlefield. The Twelfth Air Corps is insisting that the plane you are developing is too large and lacking in maneuverability. They are dissatisfied. On the other hand, it is difficult for the company to oppose the intentions of the navy." But Goto kept staring at Horikoshi with a perplexed expression on his face.

Horikoshi realized then how serious was the disturbance inside the navy over his fighter's design. After such a struggle to meet the navy's severe requirements for the 12Si fighter, it now seemed unbearable to see a change of plan sprouting. Horikoshi felt himself between the hammer and the anvil. However, as a design engineer of a company making military planes, he had no choice but to obey a change of plan coming from the navy, and within a moment he had recovered himself. He would frankly accept and try to examine scientifically the battle-tested opinions of the air corps. Why not?

He looked at Goto. "I understand now," he said. "I will think about a fighter with maneuverability as its first priority in accordance with the air corps' opinion."

On leaving Goto's office, Horikoshi immediately began examining the air corps' views. He started with the fundamental design and calculations, aiming for a light and nimble carrier-borne fighter. He calculated for two cases, one plane with retractable landing gear and another with fixed-position gear, to reduce the weight. The twenty-millimeter cannon was abolished, since it had been given 100 demerit points. The range was also reduced to give first priority to maneuverability.

In no time he came to a conclusion. From his basic calculations, the weight of the light fighters would be 15 percent less than the 12Si fighter and they would certainly be nimble. However, by any calculation, the speed of the fixed-position landing gear model was inferior to that of the 12Si fighter. The retractable landing gear model also had little merit except for a slightly higher speed. Horikoshi thought that the Twelfth Air Corps case for a light fighter could be judged by this alone.

He knew very well that the trend in fighter plane design around the world was toward greater speed, even if by only one kilometer per hour. With every country hastening the production of fast planes, it was practical to aim for a fighter with a large-horsepower engine. Moreover, considering the time it took to bring an aircraft to production, the air corps' idea of a light fighter would be left years behind the world standard, unless, of course, Horikoshi ceased to struggle with his big-engined Zero, and even then, he would have to overcome the disadvantages of the small engine that would have to be used in a light plane.

According to the Yokosuka Naval Air Corps, a medium-size airplane equipped with numerous machine guns should be used to escort bombers. But the possibility was low that such a plane could make an even fight against swarming enemy fighters. And after all, a carrier-borne fighter must be of the same long range as the 12Si carrier-borne fighter.

Though Horikoshi repeated his design calculations for the Twelfth Air Corps light fighter, he could find no point about it that was significantly better than the 12Si fighter. The comparison deepened his confidence in his creation.

His anxiety did not cease, however. Having sent his reply to the air corps' opinions through Mitsubishi to the Aeronautical Headquarters, Horikoshi remained aware that a change of plan could still be brought to the company as an order with which he would have to comply. Uneasily, he watched for the navy's reaction. None appeared. Meanwhile, the 12Si fighter's first prototype proceeded toward completion.

But the concern about a light fighter appeared to have gained strength when Horikoshi was shown the contents of 14Si and 15Si experimental development programs for fighter projects in the navy. Each project included plans for a fighter, one carrier-borne, the other an interceptor.

For the carrier-borne fighter, meant to succeed the Type 96, the specifications were:

- Purpose: As with the Type 96 carrier-borne fighter, to defeat the enemy's fighters, to destroy the enemy's bombers, to escort friendly bombers.
- Dimensions: Total width: eleven meters. Overall length: eight meters.
- Performance: Priorities are in the following order: maneuverability, climbing rate, speed, range, take-off ability, landing ability.
- Maximum speed: 518 kilometers per hour at a battle altitude of 2,000 to 6,000 meters.
- Armament and Equipment: Two sets of thirteen-millimeter machine guns and a radio direction finder besides those presently fitted in the Type 96 carrier-borne fighter.

For the interceptor fighter, the specifications were:

- Purpose: Primary purpose will be to intercept and destroy enemy bombers, and to dominate the bombers' escort fighters in air-to-air combat.
- Performance: Priorities in the following order: maximum speed (greater than that of enemy bombers by more than seventy-two kilometers per hour), climbing rate, maneuverability, range.
- Armament and Equipment: Two sets of thirteen-millimeter machine guns and two sets of 7.7-millimeter machine guns.

Both sets of specifications were clearly based on the Twelfth Air Corps' views. Implicit in them was a strong undercurrent of criticism for the 12Si fighter. The most obvious indications of this were the abolition of the twenty-millimeter cannon in both types of plane and the demand for a carrier-borne plane that would be lighter and smaller than the Type 96 carrier-borne fighter. As to the machine guns, fighters of every country in the world were tending to guns of bigger aperture. The 12Si fighter had been following this trend with its twenty-millimeter cannons in addition to the conventional 7.7-millimeter machine guns. To recede to the thirteen-millimeter or 7.7-millimeter apertures from the twenty-millimeter cannon in the 14Si and 15Si projects appeared to be evidence of the strength of criticism of the navy in adopting the twenty-millimeter gun.

The mistrust of the twenty-millimeter cannon came from concerns about the hit rate when it was installed in the wings, a low muzzle velocity, and magazines considered too small at sixty rounds each.

The move to abolish the cannons made Horikoshi angry. In meetings about the development plan for the 12Si fighter, installing twenty-millimeter machine guns had been considered from every angle. During those planning talks, Horikoshi had asked many times for confirmation of the guns from the navy. He had asked: "These new large-aperture machine guns cause no difficulties with the practicability of the fighter, do they?" And the navy had always answered "We have confidence in it." So the guns had been installed.

Horikoshi had to keep in mind, of course, that he had not actually received word from the navy to abolish the twenty-millimeter cannons from his fighter. But not including them in the 14Si and 15Si fighters appeared to be a very strong implicit criticism by the navy. At any time, that could become an order to eliminate the guns.

Horikoshi feared for the morale of his design team should they learn of his feelings. He resolved to confide only in Sone and Hatanaka. And anyway, he thought, the arrow had already left the bow. As designers, they had put their hearts and souls into a fighter that was now getting close to becoming a metal reality. It represented the cream of their abilities. They should just make the best of their enthusiasm and not be baffled by rumors and complaints.

Horikoshi's heart filled with hot emotion. He knew now that the navy expected little of the fighter he was designing, especially those pilots with battle experience. But as work on the plane advanced smoothly no order came to eliminate the cannons.

At last, in December, the structural model made of duralumin stood ready within the curtain inside the development factory. The structural model was the skeleton of the airframe only. It reminded Horikoshi of a human body without skin, with only its framework and organs showing. The duralumin airframe shone dazzlingly.

The first structural examination was carried out by the navy's officials from the Aeronautical Headquarters and the Aeronautical Establishment for three days, beginning December 26.

Meanwhile, another airframe of exactly the same structure was also under construction behind the curtains on the development factory's floor. This was the test plane to be delivered to the navy for strength tests on every part. It would be destroyed in a strength test of the total structure.

As the navy's structural examination started, officials began to note changes on the blackboards that had also been used for the examination of the wooden mockups. Watching the men working round the model, Horikoshi was touched to the core. To him, the plane was not a thing, but a creature in which life was rising, graceful and rich with precise functions inside. Although the aircraft was incomplete, he could already sense its elegance.

As the examinations finished and modifications began, the testing process got under way. The strength test structural model was delivered to the Aeronautical Establishment for strength and vibration testing. The company and the navy also met for wind tunnel testing of the spin model.

The strength test examined whether the airframe could bear the tremendous aerodynamic and inertial forces that act upon each part of the plane in the violent maneuvers of the tight turn and pulling out of a dive. The maximum possible load was to be seven times the weight of the plane, multiplied 1.8 times as a safety margin.

The vibration test consisted of applying vibration from the outside to the engine, propeller, wings, tailplanes, and control surfaces. The vibration was observed to see if it caused any vibration unique to a part of the frame. Through this test, the type of vibration that could be induced in each part of the airframe by the aerodynamic force of flight or by the vibration of the engine and propeller could be known. The types of vibration to identify were unpleasant vibrations and flutter of critical parts.

With these tests and modifications to the first skeletal model, the first trial production of the 12Si fighter came to an end at last.

Five

$\mathcal{T}$he year 1939, the fourteenth of the Showa era, began.

With the Japanese army occupying Canton and three Wuhan cities, there was still no indication that the Sino-Japanese war was coming to an end. To complicate matters, the Changkufeng incident occurred on the Soviet-Manchurian border, where Soviet and Japanese troops exchanged fire. The incident was settled by an armistice agreement, but tension along the border rose to an extreme level.

Trying to find a solution to the war, the Japanese government began to maneuver for peace with China secretly. But the effort did not easily bear fruit. Munitions aid sent by the United States, England, and the Soviet Union to the government of Chiang Kai-shek in Chungking stiffened his resistance.

The development of the 12Si carrier-borne fighter was reaching its final stages during this situation. The results of the various tests carried out at the Naval Aeronautical Establishment were favorable. Wind tunnel tests of the spin model resulted in only small modifications to the tailplane. The vibration tests had results well beyond expectations. The critical speed for wing flutter especially was estimated to be considerably higher than had been stated in Mitsubishi's report on the plane. The safety evaluation was excellent.

With such encouragement, the construction of the plane advanced rapidly. The second structural examination, concerned mainly with armaments and equipment, was carried out at the end of February. The results of that examination too were favorable, and so a complete examination by the navy was omitted.

On March 16, 1939, the first of the 12Si fighters was at last completed. Glints of moisture appeared in the eyes of Horikoshi and his fellow engineers. Eleven months had elapsed since they had submitted the aircraft's plan to the navy. They had endured much—the struggle to meet the severe restrictions, and anxiety over possible changes to the design. But now they were ready. They touched the dazzlingly shiny fuselage and the wings and stood enchanted, looking at their creation.

Next day the completion examination for the number one prototype took place. First the external form and dimensions of the completed airframe were measured, then the mobile parts. Finally, the plane was weighed on a platform scale.

To help the fighter achieve a long range unparalleled among fighters in the world at that time, and to produce the maneuverability that would enable it to dominate other light fighters in spite of being heavily equipped, Horikoshi had made tremendous efforts to keep the weight down, even by a gram. The engineers had calculated the weight beforehand. Still, they held their breath to see where the needle would stop. The needle settled at 1,565.9 kilograms. A look of relief spread over Horikoshi's face.

Among the parts already weighed, the engine was 565 kilograms, heavier than planned by forty kilograms. The three propeller blades were 144.5 kilograms, heavier by 37.5 kilograms than the two-bladed propeller originally planned. The wheels were forty-four kilograms, six kilograms heavier than the planned weight. The empty weight of the airframe—the weight remaining after subtracting those supplies from the empty weight of the plane—exceeded the planned weight by only twenty kilograms, which was a little over one percent. The excess, however, presented no difficulty.

This payload was almost twice the 372.2 kilograms of the German He-112 fighter or the 437 kilograms of the Vought V-143 fighter, sample planes purchased by the navy a year before. Considering that the weight of the German He-112 fighter was 1,686 kilograms and that of the Vought V-143, 1,578 kilograms, the 12Si fighter was amazingly light.

It was an extremely light fighter that was heavily equipped. That was an idea containing a big contradiction, but still, Horikoshi had miraculously, it seemed, managed to realize it.

Next day, the first ground operation test was carried out. Pushed by workers, the plane was rolled out from inside the curtain. Slowly it crossed the floor to the door. The door was opened, and the plane rolled outside. The sunlight of the early spring reflected dazzlingly on the airframe. The plane that been secretly built within the factory at last showed itself outside for the first time. At the center of the concrete paved open space in front of the factory, the plane was stopped and wheel blocks put in place.

Guards had warned common workers to stay out of the way beforehand. Only a small group was allowed to witness the ground test. The party included Inspector Imada and Goto, the director of the Nagoya Aircraft Works.

Engineer Takenaka entered the plane's cockpit and signaled with his hand. Two workers plugged an inertia starter in the hole and started to turn the lever by hand. The starter began to groan. The movement of the workers' hands became faster and in no time the engine had started. The propeller rotated and dust flew up. Its buzzing sound spread throughout the vicinity of the factory. The thing assembled with light metals was beating finally with life.

Takenaka waited until the oil temperature had risen and then quietly opened the throttle lever. He carefully read the gauges of the power plant, then moved the pitch lever of the constant-speed propeller and actuated the hydraulic flaps.

After a while, the propeller stopped. Takenaka stepped down to the ground. His face bore an expression of satisfaction. The test had gone smoothly. The plane was pushed back into the dimness of the development factory.

Five days later the plane was carried to the Kagamigahara Airfield in two oxcarts.

Six

On March 31, 1939, Horikoshi and other design engineers on the 12Si carrier-borne fighter project took lodgings at the Tamai Inn in the city of Gifu. Takenaka and the other engineers in charge of maintenance had been at nearby Inuyama for a week already. They were there for the inspection and adjustment of the number one prototype plane.

On that night, Horikoshi looked up at the sky from the window of the lodge. The weather forecast he had requested from the meteorological observatory said that the weather for next day, April 1, would be fine and the wind weak. To support this, the night sky seen from the window of the inn was full of stars and the white flow of the Milky Way.

Morning came. The engineers had breakfast early and headed together for the Gifu station of the Kagamigahara line. They took the shabby, creaking train and got off at Mikakino station. They traced the shortcut through bamboo bushes and fields to the airfield of the Army Supply Department.

The sky cleared up beautifully, and as predicted, there was almost no wind. "A perfect weather for the flight," the engineers kept repeating, trying to hide their concern.

A pure white tent was already stretched in front of the hangar and a wind sock was flying gently on a pole beside. They entered the hangar and gathered round the plane, which was still being adjusted. No one spoke, but in the eyes of each anxiety and expectation were mixed.

In the waiting room for pilots in the office at the back of the hangar, Harumi Aratani, the pilot, and Katsuzo Shima, the chief test pilot, who had come from the boarding house in Gifu, were waiting. Aratani was a twenty-seven-year-old who had had an unusual career. He had qualified as a test pilot through flight training in the navy after he had graduated from the Department of Electronic Engineering at Tokyo Engineering University. Shima was an ex-flight petty officer third class. He was a very experienced test pilot and had had a longer career than Aratani as a test pilot with Mitsubishi.

People concerned with the test had gathered. Lieutenant Commander Nishizawa, the full-time flight supervisor stationed at the Nagoya works, was attending the flight. Also Asada, the chief of the flight test section of the company, was present. Both men looked extremely tense.

According to the flight plan, the test flights were to be carried out in the safest way possible and in a light load condition. Communication instruments and, needless to say, the machine guns were removed. The quantity of gasoline and lubricant was also kept small. The retractable landing gear was to be kept extracted.

Finally the adjustment of the aircraft was completed. Platform scales were set under the right and left main wheels and another slid under the tail to weigh and measure the plane's center of gravity.

The weight of the aircraft was 1,928 kilograms. Then the tail was raised and measured in a level position. For the plane to be able to fly correctly, the center of gravity had to come between 20 percent and 30 percent of the mean span cord from the front edge. The tail was found to be light by this measurement, so a lead ballast of 61.5 kilograms was bound on with cloth. This completed preparations for testing.

While these preparations were underway, army flight corps training was being carried out on the airfield. The virgin flight planned, or any other special flight, could not be carried out while that was going on. The whole test party waited for the training to cease.

At last the time came. Not a plane could be seen in the sky above the airfield. Asada, the chief of the flight test section, reported to Flight Inspector Nishizawa that preparations for the test flight were complete. The door of the hangar opened with a solemn sound. The ground crew clung to the plane and pushed it with their full force. The wheels began to turn. Slowly and quietly, the plane rolled out of the hangar. Horikoshi could not keep his eyes off it as he followed Flight Inspector Nishizawa toward the tent that had been set up in front of the hangar.

In no time the plane had been stopped on the starting line. Bright sunlight reflected on the airframe. Wheel chocks were put in place. All eyes were focused on the aircraft now. It was obviously an artificial thing, reminding all of a huge, mythological bird of mysterious beauty and grace.

The wind was from the west and the velocity gauged at three meters per second. It was ideal weather for a test flight.

Straightening himself, the chief of the flight test section reported to inspector Nishizawa. "Now start the first company test flight of the number one trial production of the 12Si carrier-borne fighter." Then he went over to engineer Takenaka. "Let's start the test flight."

The recorder noted the time: 4:30 P.M.

Takenaka lowered himself into the cockpit. Two workers took the inertia starter and began to turn it forcefully. The engine started to moan, and then instantly became a high groan. The two-bladed propeller began to rotate. Horikoshi felt his body becoming hot. New life was coming into his plane.

After a while, the engine had warmed up and the rotation of the propeller rose to medium and then to high speed. The roar of the engine spread all over the airfield. The working clothes of the ground crew fluttered in the propwash. Through them pilot Shima, dressed in a flying suit, approached the plane.

Engineer Takenaka stepped down, and Shima lowered himself into the cockpit with a parachute hanging from his waist. Shima checked the control gears and the brake, and then tried the movements of rudders and flaps. Then he raised his left hand and waved right and left. Ground crews vigorously pulled on the ropes holding the wheel chocks and took them away. The plane began to move slowly.

Horikoshi felt deep emotion squeeze his heart. Like a creature, the plane he had designed was moving across the grass. The plane turned its nose left, went on the runway and moved toward the east edge.

The first test was ground gliding. The pilot applied the brake. The plane stopped, then moved again. After ten minutes of driving on the runway, the pilot brought the plane back to the starting line near the tent.

Horikoshi and the others ran up and surrounded the plane as Shima climbed down from the cockpit. He reported: "The balance of the plane in yaw, pitch, and roll, and the effectiveness of all three control rudders are fine, but the effectiveness of the brake is unsatisfactory."

The fundamental operational characteristics were good. The designers were deeply relieved.

It was the left wheel brake that was giving trouble. In addition, the temperature of the lubricant oil was high. This meant that the oil cooler was inadequate. But that wouldn't cause trouble in the test flight, they decided, so only the brake was fixed. The oil cooler would be fixed later.

At 5 P.M. pilot Shima climbed into the plane and tried ground gliding once again. This time, flight would be possible. Since it was the first flight, and because of safety considerations, only a jump flight was scheduled.

At 5:30, the signal "Start the jump flight" was given.

The plane went to the runway and moved far along to the east. Then it turned about and faced its watchers. Horikoshi and his engineers had no doubt the two-ton object would leave the ground with the pilot and fly, but still, for them an actual flight was the first real test, the edge between all the high expectations of their perfectionism and reality, and as they watched the aircraft powering up for its take off dash they felt an extreme tension. Their bodies stiffened, and their eyes concentrated on the silver object roaring alone in the distance at the end of the runway.

The wind sock showed clearly that the plane would be flying into the wind. The aircraft began its run. Horikoshi's heart began to beat hard as the plane accelerated to a great speed. He felt it was coming straight for him. Then, as its roar spread over the airfield and the wings began to glitter, the wheels left the runway. It lifted lightly, easily.

Horikoshi clenched his hand in a final fit of tension. But the plane maintained its well-balanced posture and passed in front of him at an altitude of about ten meters. It landed about 500 meters away.

Something hot suddenly squeezed Horikoshi's heart, and tears filled his eyes. He nodded speechless to fellow engineers. But they could not speak either. They too were twisting their faces in a useless effort to keep back tears.

For a plane under development, the 12Si fighter on the whole passed its first flight test very well. A brake and the oil cooler would need adjustment, but that was all.

For three days the 12Si fighter underwent modifications in Mitsubishi's hangar at Kagamigahara Airfield. The next tests began on April 5. For those tests the weather was again beautiful, with a two-kilometer wind from the southwest. This time, the company's chief flight inspector, Asada, did not come. But Supervisor Lieutenant Commander Nishizawa did, and Commander Imada. Horikoshi watched with his fellow engineers Sone and Tanaka.

At 10:25, the first test flight was started. But a minute later, the plane was forced to land with a gasping engine. The same thing happened in the afternoon test flight. Horikoshi and the others examined the problem at once. Takenaka, chief of maintenance, and another engineer, Izumi, adjusted the engine, and next day, April 6, the plane took off at 8 A.M. This time pilot Shima took it up to several hundred meters and flew for thirty-two minutes. Horikoshi watched every second of that flight.

Shima reported that the effect of the three control surfaces was extremely good and resembled closely those of the Type 96 carrierborne fighter. But the plane vibrated considerably while climbing, in level flight, and even while gliding with the engine throttled down. Shima's findings were confirmed by pilot Aratani when he flew the plane next day.

The cause of the vibration was not clear. The engineers suspected, however, that it was caused by the extended landing gear. They wondered if it was not natural for retractable gears to cause vibration when extended. The turbulence from the gear was hitting the tail plane, setting up the vibrations.

Since this first stage of flight testing had ended rather tentatively, the opportunity was taken to repair and modify the oil cooler and the shock absorber of the landing gear. The work went on for five days.

On the fourteenth of April, they decided on a flight test with the land-ing gear retracted.

The test took place in the afternoon. Horikoshi and his fellow engineers watched the takeoff anxiously. The plane left the runway. First the right and then the left landing gear was swallowed up into the underside of the plane, like arms embracing.

With the landing gear up, the streamlined appearance of the air-craft was suddenly, captivatingly apparent. Horikoshi thought it looked beautiful and was flooded with deep emotion. He had known very well what the plane would look like with its landing gear retracted. But what he was seeing now was the aircraft glittering in the sun and almost flowing, not just flying, he thought, through a clear sky.

For two hours and thirty minutes pilot Shima flew above the air-field and in its vicinity. At 5:20 P.M. he put out the landing gear and landed. He stepped out of the plane and reported at once.

The landing gear extracted very well, he said, but the left gear was a little awkward when retracting. The elevator also felt a little bit heavy at high speed. Finally, he noted that the vibrations did not stop with retraction of the gear. That put an end to the theory that the extracted gear might be the cause.

Horikoshi began to study the problem at once. He and his engi-neers suspected now that the cause might be connected with the pro-peller. They decided to try a three-bladed propeller in place of the two-bladed one used to date in the tests. The three-bladed propeller was tested on April 17, and as expected the vibrations decreased by half. The only disadvantage was an increase in weight for the aircraft of 37.5 kilograms.

With the vibration problem solved, the confidence of Horikoshi and his colleagues increased, and on April 25 they began performance and maneuverability tests with the aircraft loaded with ballast to imi-tate its regular operating weight of 2,331 kilograms. The test flight of that day produced a speed of 490 kilometers per hour. (However, actual speed was thought to be eighteen kilometers per hour faster owing to an error resulting from the position of the pitot tube.) The required speed was 500 kilometers per hour, but for an early test flight to come within ten kilometers per hour of the requirement was con-sidered splendid.

The designers and ground crew were satisfied. Tests of this num-ber one prototype plane showed clearly that it had met the severe requirements. The only problems remaining were to improve and test the response of the elevators and ailerons.

When the number one prototype plane had gone through its modifications and become almost satisfactory, Horikoshi went alone to the Aeronautical Headquarters on May 1. There he met with Wada, the chief of the engineering department, Saba, the chief of the first section, a staff member, Iwaya, and others. He then went to the Aeronautical Establishment and reported on the progress of the test flights to the director of the airframe section, Sugimoto, and Sakamaki, chief of the flight test division.

The naval officials were satisfied with the progress. They decided that Mitsubishi should continue making the flight tests and any improvements resulting and that the navy would only make the official test flight for acceptance of the prototype. This decision was significant. It meant that the navy had come to trust Horikoshi and his designers enough to let them work alone to refine the aircraft's stability and maneuverability.

Events now moved rapidly toward the day of the navy's acceptance test flight. On May 19, Wada, the chief of the engineering department, and Captain Tsukahara of Aeronautical Headquarters visited Kagamigahara Airfield for an inspection with Naota Goto, the Nagoya Aircraft Works' director. Pilot Aratani flew the plane for them. On June 5, Hanajima, the director of the Aeronautical Establishment, and other concerned officials came to inspect the new aircraft. They arranged for the official test flight dates—June 12 and 13.

But when everyone concerned came to the field on those days, the flights were canceled, owing to the bad condition of the engine. Another date was set: July 6.

At this time, the main problem left with the 12Si fighter was that the motion of the control stick was changing too much at a change of speed from low to high, making precise control of flight difficult. As a result, the pilot quickly tired while making special, high-speed flights.

A good method of solving this problem seemed to be to reduce the rigidity of the control system for the elevator. A first-step reduction of rigidity was carried out and seemed to offer a solution.

The rudders of an airplane changed their angle by a control system consisting of links and cables and air pressure over the control surfaces. In a change of angle, centrifugal force acted simultaneously with a change in direction of the aircraft, while air pressure on these surfaces changed in proportion to the square of the speed. The elevators moved up and down by pulling or pushing the control stick. Of course, the change of angle was proportional to the movement of the control stick. As with a car, the effect of moving the control stick increased rapidly with speed. A tiny shift of the stick at high speed was enough to change direction, just as a car's steering wheel need be moved only slightly at high speed to shift direction. Pilots, however, found it desirable to be able to feel the effect of the rudder in direct proportion to the movement of the control stick. This was especially desirable in a plane with a wide range of speeds. Even if the effect of the rudder should increase drastically with speed, the pilot required that effect to be felt as little as possible, and hopefully, for the difference in rudder effect and stick movement to be adjusted automatically.

At the flight test, pilot Shima complained that the effect and the heaviness of the elevator became too great at high speed. Horikoshi wondered if he could not use an automatic variable control system. He got the idea that if an elastic portion were inserted in the control system, the corresponding change in the angle of the rudder would become naturally small at high speed, and large at low speed. This way, only a moderate reduction in the rigidity of the control system was necessary to achieve precise control.

But there was an obstacle in the way. In the official requirements for the aircraft the amount of rigidity of the control system was specified. The rule, set by the army, the navy, and the Aeronautical Department of the Communications Ministry was an imitation of a rule used in foreign countries. Horikoshi wanted this rigidity to be reduced to 30 percent below the specified standard. The rigidity rule was out of date, he judged, and he made counterarguments. Fortunately, the navy supported him, but they still did not abolish the rule.

This allowed Horikoshi to carry out a second step in the reduction of the rigidity of the prototype's control system. When that indicated definitely that this was the solution to the problem, Horikoshi moved to a third reduction, which finally solved the matter.

With this solution, a date for the acceptance test flight of the prototype could be set. Much rode on this flight for Horikoshi and his engineers and Mitsubishi. It meant acceptance or rejection of the plane by the navy.

Official test flights were to be carried out by the fighter pilots of the flight test division of the Aeronautical Establishment. All were veteran navy pilots. Their opinions after a flight decided the future of the prototype plane. Not all, they thought, could be assigned a number. The pilots' very delicate "feel" for a new type of plane was also important in making a judgment. This presented some obstacle. The pilots were used to the aircraft they had flown and tended to have difficulty becoming accustomed to a new aircraft. The challenge for the prototype plane, then, was to satisfy their feelings in spite of this handicap. Otherwise, the prototype would be given an unfavorable evaluation and rejected.

The ground test started after 9 A.M. with pilot Seiichi Maki of the Aeronautical Establishment at the controls. He flew for thirty minutes. From 11:32 A.M., Lieutenant Commander Chujiro Nakano flew for forty-two minutes.

These flight tests were done with the rigidity of the control system at the second stage of reduction. With tense faces, Horikoshi and his colleagues listened to what the pilots had to say.

Pilot Seiichi Maki spoke first. "It's very nice to be able to land in spite of a maximum speed increase much greater than for the Type 96 fighter. One of the reasons must be the good landing sight. I've flown the Heinkel He-112, and the Seversky P-2PA also, but the maneuverability of this plane is much superior to those. However, the effect of the aileron is not sufficient at low speed. And the elevator is a more important problem. Its effect is too much. I'd black out if I pulled the stick as I would in an ordinary plane."

Lieutenant Commander Nakano agreed with Maki.

At these favorable opinions, relief appeared on Horikoshi's face. As to the problems with the elevator, he had already anticipated the pilots' opinions and ordered a third reduction of the rigidity of the control system. The modification was finished in time for the company's test pilot, Shima, to make a flight at 3 P.M. After him, Lieutenant Maki, Lieutenant Commander Nakano, and the pilot Aratani made more flights.

The results were just what Horikoshi had been expecting. All four fliers found the operation of the elevators perfectly satisfactory.

With such good results, the vice director of Mitsubishi, Noda, came out and the official flight test was made. The actual purpose of this test was to check the relation between the two-bladed and three-bladed propellers and vibration. First the two-bladed propeller was installed and Lieutenant Maki and Lieutenant Commander Nakano made flights. They judged the vibration too much, and so the three-bladed propeller was adopted.

Mitsubishi spent the next one and a half months making final modifications to the number one prototype. When it was finished, the navy was informed, and the date August 23 set for the second official test flight at Kagamigahara Airfield.

On that day Commander Yoshito Kobayashi from the Aeronautical Headquarters, Lieutenant Commander Yoshitake, Lieutenant Commander Nakano, and Lieutenant Maki from the Aeronautical Establishment, and five others came. The company sent Horikoshi and other engineers led by Shoda of the manufacturing division.

At 3 P.M., Lieutenant Maki and then the company pilot, Shima, made test flights. But the engine of the aircraft was so bad, they had to land right away. Adjustments were quickly made, and Lieutenant Maki and Lieutenant Commander Nakano made flights.

Again Horikoshi and his engineers waited anxiously for the pilots' opinions. But the only thing the pilots saw that needed adjusting was the aileron. That was quickly adjusted. No problems were left. The 12Si fighter was now of practical use. Horikoshi and his engineers were all smiles.

Next day, August 24, a conference was held among all those attending the official test flight in the conference room belonging to the offices of the Kagamigahara hangar. Sakamaki, the chief of the flight test division of the Aeronautical Establishment, also arrived.

At the conference, it was decided that the results of the two official test flights warranted the navy's accepting the 12Si fighter. Even so, the next day Lieutenant Commander Nakano and Lieutenant Maki made more test flights. The results were extremely good.

Fifteen days of modifications followed. These were finished on September 10, and on the thirteenth came the day when the number one prototype was to be officially received. Officials from the Aeronautical Headquarters and the Aeronautical Establishment joined Mitsubishi officials at the airfield. Pilots Shima, Maki, and Nakano carried out the confirmation flights. Its wings shining, the completely finished prototype flew above the field.

Before that day, the number one prototype had already recorded a speed of 509 kilometers per hour at 3,600 meters altitude. This was quite in excess of the navy's original requirements.

Next day, September 14, the number one prototype was rolled out of the hangar by the ground crews. When it stopped at the starting line, the crew were unwilling to let go.

Lieutenant Maki stepped into the cockpit and soon the propeller started to rotate. The plane moved onto the runway. Horikoshi and his engineers stood in a huddle together, watching as the plane accelerated for takeoff. At 9:06 A.M. it climbed into the sky. The retractable landing gear was smoothly absorbed into the airframe. When it had risen high, it banked in a circle above the airfield. Then it headed east. The men on the ground were moist-eyed as the number one prototype of the 12Si carrier-borne fighter became a shining spot and then faded out.

It had been two years since Horikoshi and his colleagues had received the official requirement plan from the navy. To obtain acceptance of Horikoshi's design, an unusual amount of testing had been done: 119 tests, 215 company and official test flights totalling forty-three hours and twenty-six minutes, and seventy hours and forty-nine minutes of ground operation.

That day, the number one prototype arrived at the Yokosuka Naval Airfield at 10 A.M.

Seven

On September 1, 1939, the German army, supported by 2,000 airplanes, invaded Poland. England and France, Poland's allies, declared war against Germany on September 3. World War II had begun.

Japan announced a policy of nonintervention in the war, but it was an extremely critical position, since Japan was allied with Germany.

In this situation, the number two prototype plane was carried to the Kagamigahara Airfield on two oxcarts. Company flight tests started on October 18.

The number two prototype had already had the modifications made to the number one prototype installed, and on September 25, after only a week of testing, it was received by the navy and flown to Yokosuka Airfield.

When he went to the Aeronautical Establishment at the end of October, Horikoshi was informed that the first flight firing test of the twenty-millimeter cannons had been made at the Establishment with the number one prototype. The plane had dived and fired at a nineteen-meter square of cloth stretched on the ground. With the cannons of both wings firing, fifty-nine bullets out of ninety had made marks on the cloth. With only one wing firing, nine bullets out of twenty made hits. These results were beyond expectations. Needless to say they were affected by the superb shooting ability of the pilot, but they were still a remarkable testimony to the excellence of the plane's stability and the design of the cannons and their equipment.

The navy had already made plans for the number three prototype to change over the installation of a new engine. In the first two prototypes Mitsubishi's Zuisei 13 engine had been mounted. The navy ordered a change to the Nakajima Aircraft Company's Sakae 12 engine for the number three prototype. The intention was to increase the horsepower. The Sakae was an excellent engine, producing a bigger output than that of the Zuisei, though it was hardly any bigger in dimension.

Horikoshi's design group had already redesigned the part that had to be changed to accept the Sakae 12 engine. With the drawings ready, the modification was complete by December of 1939.

The structural inspection of the number three prototype was carried out in the development factory in the presence of Saeki, chief of the first section of the Aeronautical Headquarters, Sugimoto, the director of the airframe division of the Aeronautical Establishment, and twenty other people from the navy. The inspection went off without a problem. The plane was then transported to the Kagamigahara Airfield and company flight tests started December 28.

As 1940 (the fifteenth year of Showa) began, the flight test of the number three prototype went on. The effect of changing to the new Sakae 12 engine was remarkable. The aircraft recorded a high speed of more than 533 kilometers per hour at an altitude of 4,500 meters— far exceeding the 500 kilometers per hour at 4,000 meters laid out in the original requirements, and in addition, outclassing any other fighter in the world.

Independently of each other, the navy and the army had been doing speed comparisons with a Heinkel He-112 from Germany, and an American Vought V-143, respectively. The Heinkel had a maximum speed of 444 kilometers per hour at 3,600 meters, and at the same altitude, the Vought V-143 had a speed of 426 kilometers per hour. These were first-class planes, but their speeds didn't match that of the Type 96 carrier-borne fighter, and came nowhere near the Zero's.

Overjoyed at these comparisons, the navy hastened the first official test flight for the Sakae-powered number three prototype.

The test was held January 18–19, 1940. As before, Lieutenant Maki piloted for the Aeronautical Establishment. He took the first test flight, and was followed by others. The flights were observed by Wada, the director of the engineering department of the Aeronautical Establishment Headquarters, Kira, the director of the Establishment's flight test division, and Rear Admiral Minami, chief inspector for the Nagoya region.

The results led immediately to the navy adopting the number three prototype with its Sakae 12 engine, and on the twenty-fourth of January it was flown to Yokosuka Airfield, a flight taking one hour and thirty-five minutes.

Over the next period, the navy received another three prototypes of the 12Si fighter. In the number four prototype, the twenty-millimeter magazines were changed from seventy-five to ninety rounds each.

By that time, news of the Zero's incredible performance had spread to the navy's aviation corps in China, and a clamor rose to have the new fighter sent to them. The Japanese air forces in China saw the amazing new fighter as a means of breaking a technical stalemate that had developed in their battles with the Chinese air force. Though three Wuhan cities had fallen, and an air base at Hankow had been secured, the Chinese air force had recovered its strength completely. Japanese bombers raiding the capital of Chungking were met by swarms of fighters that were inflicting more and more damage because, in spite of a remarkable range, the Type 96 carrier-borne fighter could not escort as far as Chungking. The Zero looked to be the solution. It had the necessary range and also the superior dogfighting ability of the Type 96. Test results of the 12Si fighter, revealed to the naval air force in Japan, only increased the demand for it to be put into service immediately.

Naval Aeronautical Headquarters, however, did not respond right away. In spite of the 12Si fighter's excellent test results, the Headquarters regarded it still as an experimental plane, needing more testing. The requests from the continent were so strong, however, that the program of improvements and testing had to be hastened along.

A prime concern of the Aeronautical Establishment's experiments with the 12Si fighter was to repeat research into change of pitch problems with its constant-speed propeller during fighting maneuvers. The constant-speed propeller was designed to respond to changes in flight speed and automatically adjust the blade angle of the propeller so that the propeller's speed remained constant. However, it was observed that the rotation of the propeller became excessive when speed was increased sharply. Obviously the propeller blade's angle of change could not follow the change of speed.

The Aeronautical Establishment was intensely investigating this problem when, on March 11, an unexpected and serious accident occurred at Oppama Airfield. On that morning Lieutenant Maki piloted the number three prototype of the 12Si fighter, while Masumi Okuyama, a test pilot of the flight test division of the Aeronautical Establishment, took off in the number two prototype. Both pilots were investigating the pitch change situation in their planes with the constant-pitch propeller.

Okuyama was a former flight petty officer first class of the navy who had transferred to the Aeronautical Establishment. He was a skilled test pilot, with 2,000 flying hours and many flight tests to his credit.

On that day, Okuyama's plane was to make two diving tests from 1,500 meters down to 500, with the second dive at an angle of fifty degrees. Then suddenly, around 10:30 P.M., during the first test dive, a strange sound rang around the airfield. People looked up and saw that something terrible had happened to Okuyama's number two prototype.

The aircraft had exploded in the air. People shouted in dismay as they saw that the plane had completely disintegrated. The engine section fell rapidly as the wings and parts of the fuselage fell glittering through the sky to land on the grass of the airfield, where they shone gorgeously like fragments of the sun.

Above, a parachute opened. Sighs of relief came from the people looking up. Lieutenant Commander Chuujiro Nakano, the senior pilot of the flight test section, clung onto one of the airfield's tripod binoculars and focused on the figure of test pilot Okuyama. His head and hands were hanging limply as he descended in the straps of the chute.

Nakano checked Okuyama's body through the binoculars. There was no sign of a gash or the color of blood. Was it that his bones had been smashed to powder by the impact of the explosion? Or had he had time to escape before? Nakano wondered if Okuyama were not just unconscious.

Slowly the parachute came down in the clear sky. Then, at 300 meters above the ground, Okuyama's hands were seen to move a little. "He's alive!" Nakano shouted joyfully as he peered through the lens.

But a moment later, Okuyama suddenly parted from the parachute and fell, rotating. Mournful shouts broke out in the watching crowd below.

The principal observers, including Nakano, piled into an automobile nearby and hurried to the north end of the airfield.

Okuyama's body lay face down on the shoal of the beach. When he was held up, his eyes were loosely closed and the seal of death was already on his face. Pilots and ground crew crowded round him. The calm waves of an early spring sea washed around the corpse.

Nakano and others lifted up Okuyama's body from the sea and carried it to the beach, where it was loaded in a car. Then it was taken to a sickroom of the Establishment. An autopsy was made by a military surgeon, who determined that the cause of death was a fall from the height of 300 meters.

Okuyama's parachute was recovered from the beach right away and examined, but no abnormality could be found except that the fastener was open. Clearly that was the reason Okuyama had parted from his chute and fallen. But nothing could be found wrong with the fastener. It clasped tightly and properly when closed. It could not have opened naturally.

Many people beside Nakano had been watching the figure of Okuyama through binoculars immediately after the accident. They had also witnessed Okuyama moving his hands slightly as he descended. He was certainly alive then, but that only deepened the mystery of his sudden fall. It was possible that he had partly regained consciousness and had unclasped the fastener thinking he was on the ground. No other explanation seemed to fit.

Okuyama's family came in haste. His body remained in the Establishment that night for the ceremony of the vigil, then it was cremated. His remains were returned home in a chest provided by his mourning family.

The Nagoya Aircraft Works had been informed at once of the midair disintegration of the number two prototype. The news was a big surprise to the director of the works and everyone concerned. Horikoshi left the same day for the airfield.

At 8:30 the next morning he presented himself at the flight test division of the Aeronautical Establishment and offered his condolences. Then he heard the whole story of the incident. It was of course a very serious matter. The plane had been accepted after many flight tests and modifications, and had left the hands of Mitsubishi Heavy Industries, Ltd. Still, it was considered the company's responsibility to determine the cause of the accident in cooperation with the navy.

Horikoshi attended a conference on the accident which lasted from morning to the afternoon. Then in the evening he attended the farewell service for the pilot Okuyama at the Establishment. At the ceremony, he hung his head before the spirit of the departed. He felt himself a little cowed by the loss of a precious human life in a plane he had designed. But that only made it all the more urgent to investigate the cause of the accident thoroughly and make the 12Si fighter as perfect as possible. That was the only way to make amends to the lost test pilot Okuyama.

At the next day's conference, investigation of the cause of the accident was the first priority. Considerable numbers of people had witnessed the accident, but all had only looked up at the sky after they had heard the sounds of disintegration. They had only seen fragments of wings and the fuselage scattering in the sky. There was only one person, a worker at the Establishment named Miyano, who had clearly witnessed the instant of the plane's breakup.

Miyano had happened to gaze up at Okuyama's plane just before the accident had occurred. According to him, Okuyama's plane was in the course of making a dive from 1,500 meters at an angle of fifty to fifty-five degrees when, at four or five hundred meters, the plane suddenly emitted a strange noise. The plane made no attempt to pull up before there was a loud bang and it blew apart. However, it all happened so quickly, Miyano could not tell the part of the plane where the destruction had started. The investigators could not determine that either from his testimony.

The fragments of the number two prototype had been gathered in the third factory of the airframe division of the Establishment. The engine, engine mount, and propeller had been recovered from the sea. Other parts were picked off the airfield. But the constant-speed propeller governor, the carburetor, and the instrument panel appeared to have fallen into the sea and been lost.

Horikoshi looked over these enormous fragments. They were spread all over the concrete floor of the factory, and they were so terribly destroyed that it was hard to bear looking at them. He was shown a figure that showed the distribution of the fall of fragments, but it seemed to him that it might be difficult to identify the clue that would indicate stages of the plane's destruction in the air.

The conference proceeded in a grave atmosphere. Unless the cause of the damage was identified and an improvement designed, the 12Si carrier-borne fighter could not be accepted by the Navy.

Engineer Kiyoshi Matsudaira, in charge of vibration study at the airframe division, testified at the conference. "According to the results of the vibration ground test on the real plane and on the flutter model in the wind tunnel, this plane had no risk of flutter below 1,110 kilometers per hour."

Flutter is a phenomenon in which aerodynamic force causes destructively violent vibration of the main wing, tails, control surfaces, or fuselage, independently or together, when the aircraft exceeds a certain speed. The occurrence of flutter depends on the shape, rigidity, and distribution of the mass of each part.

"However," Matsudaira went on, "in cases of flutter in the past, only main wings were destroyed in an occurrence of main wing flutter, only tails in an occurrence of tail flutter. I have never known all the parts of a plane to be torn apart as is the case here. I intend to make a survey based on the distribution of the fragments, but I'm not sure a conclusion can be reached."

Then engineer Azuma, an official in charge of the strength test for airplanes, testified. "As for this airplane," he said, "the front body is the weakest of all statically. The number one and two prototypes were restricted to an acceleration to 6.8 gs [the requirement was 7.0 gs]. However, the plane had the planned safety margin of 1.8 times, therefore it is not the case that the plane would break up in pulling up at 6.8 gs."

In due course, the field survey discovered that the arm of the mass balance weight of the elevator of Okuyama's plane had been broken. The mass balance weight had been lost before the flight. An investigation based on this fact was vigorously led by Matsudaira. Wind tunnel flutter tests were made almost every day, and finally an official decision with regard to the cause of the accident was given. It was based on the fact that the mass balance weight of the elevator had been lost before the flight. Matsudaira concluded that when the plane's speed had increased during its deep dive, flutter had broken out on the elevator, which had lost its mass balance weight. The vibration induced a violent vibration to the whole airframe. As a result, the airframe was destroyed.

But many doubts were left by this explanation. "It is unconvincing that the flutter of the elevator could snatch off the engine from the body and totally destroy the airframe," stated one investigator, and based on this view, another cause was mentioned: irregularities of the pitch angle among the blades of the constant speed propeller. An over-rotation of the propeller, leading to violent vibration, could have been caused by the pitch angle being too small because the change of pitch had taken place too slowly. The violent vibrations resulting would in turn have induced a violent vibration to the whole airframe. As a result, the whole airframe would have been destroyed.

The investigation accepted, however, the conclusions of Matsudaira after all. As a result, the arm of the mass balance weight of the elevator was strengthened for all planes, including those under construction or already received.

Important data emerged from the investigation of the accident. It had always been thought that the new material duralumin would develop fractures and become fragile after a certain time (time fractures), and that the duralumin main spar was especially likely to fatigue because of the load it received repeatedly during flight. But microscope investigations of the broken surface revealed that the main spar had been broken suddenly by flutter, and not by time fracture or fatigue. Still, it was thought necessary to investigate again the life span of the duralumin main structure. The life span of the main spar especially came under scrutiny, and the Establishment began to carry out tests to study this by a program of repeated loads for a long time.

The accident also raised questions about the possibility of extreme acceleration and centrifugal forces causing the plane to disintegrate. To measure how much and how often these forces had acted on the plane, pilots led by Lieutenant Manbei Shimokawa, fighter squadron leader of the Yokosuka Naval Air Corps, attached an auto-recording accelerometer to a plane and then repeatedly engaged in intense mock air combat against a Type 96 carrier-borne fighter or another 12Si fighter. As a result, it was found that planes before number twenty-one would have to be restricted to fifty hours of air combat time with a large safety margin. Of course, the air combat time of the number two prototype when it had disintegrated had been much less than fifty hours, which made it obvious that extremes of acceleration and centrifugal force had nothing to do with its destruction.

With the cause of the accident and measures to repair it clearly determined, the 12Si carrier-borne fighter was ready at last for production, and planes began to flow smoothly out of the Nagoya Aircraft Works.

Eight

During 1940, the German invasion of the European continent continued. Germany captured Denmark and Norway in April, and in May Germany brought the Netherlands and Belgium to their knees. German troops also broke through the Maginot Line on the German-French border with a vigorous attack by tanks and planes. In no time they had invaded French territory. Paris fell on June 14, and France surrendered.

Within her own sphere of interest, Japan's situation was getting more and more complicated. On the Soviet-Manchurian border in the previous year an incident at Nomonhan had taken place following the earlier one at Changkufeng. A cease-fire had been declared before long, but a strong concern arose among Japan's military leaders that total war might break out with the Soviets. In China, the United States was actively giving military aid to the Kuomintang government in Chungking. The Chinese conflict was expanding beyond anyone's expectations and it appeared that it would be prolonged with no prospect of settlement. Meanwhile, Japan's membership in the Anti-Comintern pact with Italy and Germany was leading it into increasing isolation internationally.

In China, the Japanese navy's aviation corps worked in cooperation with the army. The corps was mainly deployed in central and south China. However, the Chinese air force had receded beyond the range of the highly successful Type 96 carrier-borne fighter, and with recovered strength, its resistance was becoming increasingly effective, especially against the unescorted Type 96 land-based torpedo bombers being used to bomb Chungking.

On June 18, 1940, Lieutenant Tamotsu Yokoyama, squadron leader of the Omura Naval Air Corps of the Nagasaki District, was suddenly transferred to the Yokosuka Naval Air Corps together with subordinates chosen for their excellent flying technique. Yokoyama was a very good fighter pilot. He had served in the aircrew of the aircraft carrier *Soryu* and also had gained battle experience in China.

All he was told about his transfer to the Yokosuka Naval Air Corps was that it was for an "important mission." It wasn't until he went to pay his respects to his new superior that he finally learned why he had been sent. He was to organize one squadron of the new 12Si fighters for operational testing by the Aeronautical Headquarters and the Yokosuka Naval Air Corps. Then he was to take the squadron to China as quickly as possible.

Yokoyama had been hearing rumors about the 12Si fighter. It was said to be an all-purpose fighter of great speed and extreme maneuverability with a long range, and large twenty-millimeter aperture cannons. It was said to have been produced to the navy's next-to-impossible requirements by the makers of the Type 96 carrier-borne fighter, Mitsubishi's Nagoya Aircraft Works.

Yokoyama felt great joy at this new duty, but he was also immediately tense with its heavy load of responsibility. He informed his men of the mission right away and they all went out to look at the 12Si fighters.

They looked over their new aircraft with eyes already enchanted. With its good style, the Type 96 carrier-borne fighter had surprised these pilots when first they had set eyes on one, but the 12Si was so refined, it was graceful. Though bigger, it looked full of agility. Yokoyama got in a plane and took off. At once he recognized the excellent performance—the high speed, the maneuverability. It felt more like a part of his body than a plane.

He immediately began organizing his squadron. He requested Lieutenant Manbei Shimokawa, of the Yokosuka Naval Air Corps, to give him more pilots to add to his original group.

While doing this, Yokoyama learned that it was an unprecedented act to send a plane to the front line while it was still being operationally tested. The decision had been taken in spite of considerable opposition by aviation technicians in the navy. The decision meant that the superiority of the 12Si fighter had not been officially accepted, and that only exceptionally strong demands from the front line had made the navy agree to sending the new fighter. Yokoyama was told to get to China as quickly as possible. That meant training himself and his subordinates in the flying techniques of the new fighter to the point where they would be skilled enough for action.

Yokoyama's group had plunged into an intense program of drills and practice when they were joined by another new 12Si squadron, led by Lieutenant Commander Saburo Shindo. Shimokawa also had a squadron, and it was his squadron that ran into new problems with the new fighter.

On June 25, 1940, Shimokawa's group was carrying out operational tests and tried one for high altitude. The number six plane of the squadron experienced a drop in fuel pressure and had to give up the climb at 7,800 meters. The number four plane, however, got to 10,300 meters in thirty-four minutes twenty-five seconds, in spite of also developing minor trouble with its engine. It was reported that it would have been possible to climb yet farther if the engine had remained good.

Number four's engine trouble and the drop in fuel pressure in number six plane were studied. It was found that the fuel, warmed on the ground, had had no time to cool in the fighter's very fast climb. As a consequence the fuel had vaporized, blocking the fuel pipe. The problem was solved by using a special fuel, 92-octane, then in trial production.

There were other problems revealed in this training session. In repeated firing tests of the twenty-millimeter cannons during level flight, zooming, and diving, the automatic feed sometimes caused trouble during acceleration. This problem was solved by modifying the exhausted cartridge discharge tube for the twenty-millimeter cannons. In all, the tests expended 20,396 rounds of twenty-millimeter cannon ammunition.

At high speed, the streamlined drop fuel tank, the first of its kind in the world, had a tendency not to detach when required. It was found that it would certainly do so if speed dropped to 330 kilometers per hour. But even with the drop tank attached, it became clear that the plane's superior performance in dogfighting was little affected.

A final problem discovered in operational and training flights was that the cylinder temperature became too high during air combat or when climbing at full power. No solution had been found to this when Yokoyama was suddenly ordered to proceed to China.

Only ten days had elapsed since his transfer to the Yokosuka Naval Air Corps. He protested. The new fighter still had problems that it wouldn't do to be trying to solve on the front line, he said. The Aeronautical Establishment agreed. He would have to go, but they assigned a group of technical officers, Lieutenant Shoichi Takayama of the airframe division, Lieutenant Osamu Nagano of the powerplant division, and engineer Sotoji Inzei of the armament division to join him at his squadron's base in Hankow. In addition, ten ground crews specializing in the 12Si fighter were to be sent along.

At the beginning of July Yokoyama left for China. He took off from Yokosuka base with a group of six 12Si fighters. They refueled at Omura field in Nagasaki Prefecture. Then they crossed the sea in one hop ending at Shanghai. The hop to Shanghai from Japan was a record for a fighter and proved how superior was the long range performance of the 12Si. At Shanghai the planes refueled and headed for Hankow, following the Yangtze River.

They had just passed Anqing along the way when dense clouds blocked their way. In no time the group was flying in heavy rain. Yokoyama was afraid they'd lose direction in the cloud and ordered the group to get below it. They circled down until close to the surface of the river. However, the circling caused the hands of the compasses to start to spin. To get to Hankow they had only to fly upriver, but the Yangtze was so wide at that point, Yokoyama could not tell which was the right direction. Yokoyama started to worry. Failure to deliver the brand new fighters would be a serious letdown to the front-line men in Hankow. Just then, he spotted a small sandbank island. From that, he knew he would be able to tell which way the river below him was running. One end of the islet was round, the other sharp from the river's flow. The round side was obviously upriver.

The group chose this direction and flew on, skimming the water. At last, Hankow field came into view. Six 12Si fighters extracted their landing gear and prepared to land. The pilots could see considerable numbers of people lining the runway and looking up at them. Some were waving. They estimated the crowd at 500 or 600 persons.

One by one the aircraft landed. Instantly, each was surrounded by cheering people. Among them could be seen Rear Admiral Tamon Yamaguchi, commander of the First United Air Corps. Rear Admiral Takijiro Onishi, commander of the Second United Air Corps, was there, too. From this reception, Yokoyama realized how great were the expectations of the front-line people. It was lucky he had managed to arrive safely with the planes.

The excitement at the airfield did not subside. Pilots and ground crews would not stop staring at the six new fighters. Yokoyama and his men were peppered with questions.

Next day, Yokoyama resumed the hard training for combat. Meanwhile, the technical officers assigned by the Naval Aeronautical Technical Establishment had arrived and got to work on the unsolved problems discovered in the training and operational testing in Japan.

After a few days, however, Yokoyama was summoned by the commanders of the two united air corps, Rear Admiral Tamon Yamaguchi and Rear Admiral Takijiro Onishi. They ordered him to make a sortie as soon as possible with his six 12Si fighters. He would be escorting land-based torpedo bombers. These bombers were still raiding Chungking without fighter escort. Mounting losses from the Chinese fighter defense were upsetting the officers.

Yokoyama, however, did not feel ready. "I am sorry to have to reply to an order," he began, "but the 12Si carrier-borne fighter still has unsolved problems. This is the advent of a new fighter, and so if our first campaign has poor results, not only will the morale of our own men suffer but also the enemy's will rise. Please give us more time. We will make the fighter fit for operation. Then we can join the battle and achieve victory at a stroke."

Both rear admirals accepted Yokoyama's sincere request. He was ordered to solve the problems and join the air battle as quickly as possible, even by a day.

Hankow had an extremely hot summer. In the burning heat, Yokoyama's group continued tests and training while the technical members labored on improvements, particularly a successful solution to the problem of the overheating cylinders. Meanwhile, another nine 12Si fighters arrived from the Yokosuka Naval Air Corps under the command of Lieutenant Saburo Shindo. This made a total of fifteen 12Si fighters at the Hankow Air Base.

At the end of July, it was felt that the 12Si fighter had had all its technical problems solved and was ready for official adoption by the navy. The new aircraft was named after the end of the year Kigen 2,600 as the type Rei (Zero) carrier-borne fighter Model II.

"The carrier-borne fighter Type Zero." Yokoyama and the others kept on looking at the plane that had already become a part of their flesh.

From about that time, Yokoyama and Shindo were often called to the united air corps commanders' offices. "What are you doing? Are you still not confident enough for battle? Bombers are being heavily damaged," the commanders scolded, with bitter expressions.

But both pilots could only answer, "Please give us more time."

It was only one month since Yokoyama and the other pilots had first seen the new fighters. The plane's high performance took some getting used to in order to get the maximum from its capabilities. Though they had been training hard, one month was still not enough.

In the hot sun of Hankow's summer, the training went on more intensely than ever. A cloth of the same size and outline as a real plane was spread on the ground. The planes practiced strafing it. The pilots' shooting improved rapidly, and they became confident of their ability in battle.

By mid-August, Yokoyama and Shindo also felt their pilots were ready for a sortie, and on August 19, 1940, twelve Zeros under Yokoyama took off from Hankow as escorts for fifty-four torpedo bombers raiding Chungking. The united air corps commanders were among the many people who watched the fighters go.

In the bombers, the crews wore bright expressions. At last they had an escort for their whole mission. The men smiled and waved at Yokoyama and his pilots. A reconnaissance plane had reported that about thirty fighters were waiting for the torpedo bombers over Chungking. They would take off from their airfields when the bombers approached. "Thirty to twelve" Yokoyama murmured to himself. These were the odds chosen for the Zero's first combat mission. But he thought that with the Zero's performance and the quality of his pilots, they at least could not be miserably defeated.

The raiding bombers and their escorts approached Chungking together in a great roar of engines. The land-based torpedo bombers started bombing, the flashes of explosions and dust clouds spreading under them. Yokoyama's group waited for the enemy planes to intercept. But to their surprise, none appeared. There were not even any planes on the airfield. Yokoyama carefully searched for the enemy. In the end, he had to return home without a shot fired.

Next day twelve Zeros under Lieutenant Shindo joined another group of raiders heading for Chungking. Again, Chinese fighters were nowhere to be seen, and the escorts returned without fighting. The Japanese surmised that the Chinese had got wind of the new fighters and were completely avoiding them.

It was all quite strange—and wonderful. It had never happened that the torpedo bombers could fly to Chungking, meet no interception, and all return safely. At the same time, it was also an aviation first in the world for their single-seat fighter escorts to be making nonstop a 1,500 kilometer return journey to Chungking and back in formation.

On September 12, Lieutenant Yokoyama led a group of twelve fighters as escort for twenty-seven bombers on a Chungking raid. Again, the Chinese failed to appear, and this time Yokoyama flew inland as far as fuel permitted, trying to find them. On the way home the Zeros strafed the facilities of Chonmachow Airfield.

Yokoyama and his pilots became irritated. Their main purpose was to fight other fighters and they couldn't prove the superiority of their new Zeros until they met some. It was at that point that surprising information came from Chungking about the whereabouts of the Chinese fighters. What they were doing was evacuating the Chungking area before the Japanese arrived. After the bombers had left, the Chinese planes reappeared. They would circle over the city a few times, then withdraw. That appearance was enough, however, to justify the Chinese propaganda claim that their air force had inflicted heavy damage on the Japanese air corps and chased them away.

With this information, Yokoyama and Shindo met to discuss their tactics. They decided to trick the Chinese air force. The trick would be to pretend to leave the Chungking area with the bombers after the raid. The evacuated Chinese fighters would then make their appearance. Meanwhile, with careful attention to timing, the Zeros would turn around and rush back to Chungking, taking advantage of their high speed. They would then get the contact with the Chinese fighters they wanted.

Yokoyama decided to carry out the operation as soon as possible and next day, September 13, thirteen Zeros under Lieutenant Shindo and Lieutenant j.g. Ayao Shirane prepared to sortie from Hankow Airfield. The operation plan was shown to the tense pilots. They took off successively with the land-based bombers, and were joined by a land-based reconnaissance plane to search for the Chinese fighters. Yokoyama watched the figures of the Zero fighters in the hot, sunny sky with a sweating forehead. The glittering planes soon became small dots in the sky and faded out.

Nine

Thirteen Zero fighters under the command of Lieutenant Saburo Shindo and Lieutenant j.g. Ayao Shirane were escorting the land-based torpedo bomber units of Nakamura, Nakai, Yamagata, Terajima, and Nanba under General Commander Suzuki along the Han-shui River towards Chungking.

Lieutenant Saburo Shindo was a distinguished fighter pilot with a lot of battle experience escorting bomber raids against the Shanghai, Nanking, and Canton regions. He had piloted the Type 95 and Type 96 carrier-borne fighters, and others besides.

He remembered the days he had flown the Type 96 carrier-borne fighter, flying with land-based torpedo bombers. The Type 96 fighter was an excellent machine, high in all performances besides those of fighting. But to escort bombers, its engine had to be throttled to the limit to keep steady with the bomber's slow speed, since the fighter's cruising speed was too high. That caused engine trouble, though not often, and pilots would have to return to base against their will. To avoid this difficulty, it had been suggested that the fighters should fly in snakes. But that maneuver had the risk of being mistaken for an enemy attack by nervous bomber crews.

Flying in snakes wasn't necessary with the Type Zero fighter. Shindo had to throttle the engine of course, but during operational test flights, the Zero had been improved to be able to fly smoothly with the bombers. It was an excellent plane, and Shindo got an immense feeling of satisfaction listening to the rhythmical engine.

Still, no matter how well the Zero performed in tests, Shindo shared Yokoyama's and the other pilots' irritation at the lack of a real dogfight—the only way to confirm the Zero's remarkable capabilities. There was some risk in that, too, because it wasn't unthinkable that defects could yet show up in combat in a newly developed fighter.

Today, then, was a gamble for Shindo. This was the day to finally prove the Zero's excellence. To achieve that, it was very important that the Chinese fighters behaved as had been reported to Yokoyama and him—evacuating when the Japanese raiding force approached, then returning to circle in the empty skies after the raiders had left. For success, Shindo would have to be correct in calculating when the Chinese fighters would reappear over the city so he could make a rapid turn back in time to catch them.

The sky was beautifully clear that day. The flow of the Han-shui was blue, and then rows of mountains like the ripples of a crust began to spread below him, their peaks and valleys showing clearly. The rows of mountains ended and a plain was seen. Chungking lay beyond, 405 nautical miles from Hankow. The hands of Shindo's watch already showed 1:30 P.M. Shindo quickly scanned the sky around. As usual, there was no sign of the Chinese air force.

As the raiding group approached the town, antiaircraft fire rose like a reversed heavy rain. The air around filled with flashes and smoke and the sound of explosions. Each of the bombers in the Nakamura, Nakai, and Yamagata units began bombing. Bombs plunged glittering into Chungking, which lay between two rivers. Faint fires flashed everywhere in the town and points of black smoke sprouted. In no time the fires spread and smoke rose in great black pillars. Meanwhile, bombers of the Terajima and Nanba units flew over Hait'unghsi, the southern part of Chungking, and bombed heavily. Their targets were military factories and rows of storehouses that had been missed before. Now black smoke and fire erupted from those buildings.

The sky above Chungking was covered with puffs of smoke from antiaircraft fire and black smoke that rose thickly from the ground. In keeping with the plan, the Zero fighters kept circling as usual above Chungking, watching for the Chinese fighters.

The bombing ended. As the bombers began to turn back one by one toward Hankow, Shindo gathered his wingmen and quickly left too, following the bombers. His information about the Chinese fighters was that ten minutes after the bombing had ended, they would start to appear over Chungking. That was when Shindo planned to make his turn back for the city.

The combined group of fighters and bombers headed for Hankow. Shindo kept his eyes on his watch. When the hands pointed exactly to 2:20 P.M., he signalled his men to turn. He was fifty kilometers from Chungking. The thirteen fighters headed back toward the city at an altitude of 3,000 meters and a speed of 300 kilometers per hour.

Shindo's heart was beating rapidly. Would the Chinese fighters be there? He paced their approach by his watch. Before he got too close, he made his men take up combat formation. Then they continued a stealthy approach from the east.

"Be there!" Shindo kept thinking to himself. He ran his eyes over the clear sky toward the city. Suddenly his eyes caught glittering points far beyond. The point-like objects were moving slowly toward Chungking from the southwest. "There!" he shouted in his mind.

He pointed the direction to his vice commander, Lieutenant j.g. Shirane's plane. It seemed from Shirane's nods inside his canopy that he had already seen them.

Shindo directed his planes to a lower altitude and led them to the north. The enemy fighter's movements could be seen more clearly if the Japanese placed the Chinese against the brightness to the south, while putting themselves in the north and a little below the enemy fighters. It was a tactic effective against fighters in large numbers.

Shindo studied the bright spots of the fighters flying toward Chungking. There were nine groups, each consisting of three moving in a precise geometric pattern. They totalled twenty-seven. Shindo rapidly calculated the odds. Thirteen against twenty-seven. The enemy more than twice outnumbered them. Still, he was not uneasy. He only longed for the fight to begin.

He decided to increase altitude and come into position behind the Chinese. The nose of his plane rose suddenly and his men followed. Drop tanks were detached from the underside of the fuselages. They dropped glittering toward the earth.

From the steady, precise formation of the Chinese aircraft, Shindo guessed that they were unaware of his approach. Apparently they had not imagined that his squadron would make a stealthy return to Chungking.

The altitude of the Zeros increased rapidly. The squadron took up a position about 1,000 meters above the Chinese formation. It was a good position, Shindo thought. The combat could be forced in their favor if they took a higher position and got in the first blow by a charge from above.

Guiding his men, Shindo began to approach the Chinese formation below. It was about 8,000 meters to the Chinese fighters. Shindo increased speed to 400 kilometers per hour and dived slightly to one side in their direction. He was afraid his pilots' shooting would be inaccurate if their speed increased too much.

As the distance closed rapidly, the Chinese fighters saw the approaching fighters. They broke formation and scattered, increasing their speed. The aircraft were Polikparov I-15s, and I-16s, the pride of the Soviet Union.

Shindo dashed to the lead plane of the formation. He judged it must be the commander's plane. He pulled the twenty-millimeter cannon trigger. The aircraft absorbed tracers, but no white smoke came out. Shindo tried to correct his position, but to his surprise, he was going so fast he passed over the enemy. Quickly he pulled up.

All round him ferocious combats had broken out between the fighters of both sides. Getting himself into a good position, he poured bullets into an enemy fighter nearby. White smoke instantly began pouring from the fuel tank. It put down its nose and dropped. But Shindo already had other thoughts. He pulled back on his stick and zoomed up above the battle.

It was his duty to watch the combat generally and be in a high position to make commands. Naturally, he was ready to attack if he saw his men at a disadvantage, or enemy fighters came up at him.

Below him the battling planes zoomed and dived amid a spreading roar of engines and machine guns flashing like shooting stars. Shindo watched the dazzling movements of fighters on both sides. Then he gasped at the strange sight developing below.

In straight lines or curves the figures of the planes ran through the sky. The lines crisscrossed and tangled with each other. But in the quickness of the movements, two kinds could be clearly distinguished. The I-15s and I-16s were moving slowly by comparison to the Zeros flashing past them. The difference in the speeds was great, and those planes being destroyed and going down were all I-15s and I-16s.

Then a strange thing happened. The quickness of the Japanese fighters somehow forced the Chinese fighters to bunch together. The Zeros surrounded them and began to pour bullets into the massed planes. One by one the Chinese fighters went down. This sight reminded Shindo of a net cast over a school of fishes. Some fighters escaped the net but they were quickly chased and shot down by the Japanese fighters. Three parachutes opened in the sky, like dandelion fuzz.

The bunched Chinese fighters gradually lost altitude and the whole battle shifted slowly to the west of Chungking. Shindo reduced his own altitude and kept on watching from above. It was a fierce combat.

One fighter escaped below and his men chased after it at high speed. When they reached an altitude of fifty or sixty meters above ground, the enemy fighter failed to make a turn, crashed on its nose, and shattered. It must have been hit by the powerful twenty-millimeter cannon. Another plane's wing was shattered and it dropped; another was suddenly enveloped in flames and went down. Yet another plunged in a spiral, leaving a trace of white smoke.

Shindo was not sure how long the battle had lasted by the time he realized that the only fighters left in the sky were Zeros. They kept on circling at high speed, their pilots still in a fever of battle excitement.

Shindo was amazed at the ferocity of the air battle. His squadron had won a complete victory. Though his men had scattered all over the sky looking for surviving enemy fighters, none could be found. Looking at his watch, Shindo saw it read 2:40 P.M. The battle had lasted ten minutes.

Shindo felt his heart warming. The air battle that had just taken place before him demonstrated clearly that the Zero fighter was a performer of an excellence far beyond their wildest expectations. He also saw that the hard training of his pilots had allowed them to give full play to the plane's capabilities.

Lieutenant Shindo began to gather up his wingmen. Four planes of his were circling above Chungking. Shindo turned everyone toward the meeting point fifty kilometers east of Chungking, where they had turned back from the bombers to attack the Chinese fighters.

Five Zeros headed by Shindo arrived at this point, and they circled slowly at 3,000 meters, following their plan. One by one, spot-like figures appeared at the corner of the western sky. Presently Shindo had nine fighters with him.

He decided the other four must have gone off on a chase. Gathering his men into formation, he headed for Ichang Airfield. Ichang was about half way to Hankow on the Yangtze River. It had been chosen as a point where the fighters could refuel if they had expended too much in combat. Approaching the base, ten fighters put down their landing gear and one by one landed, headed by Shindo.

The ground crews eagerly attended the planes. Meanwhile, the pilots climbed down and came running to Shindo. Their faces were shining bright with excitement. But Shindo kept watching the corner of the sky silently.

He had not seen any of his men shot down in the battle. But considering the number of the enemy, more than twice the Zeros, he was still anxious that four planes had not appeared. Seeing his expression, his men also took to searching the sky.

"Returned!" The voices of his men were joyous. One tiny figure of a plane appeared in the bright sky. Three more appeared as bright spots following it.

Shindo felt hot tears in his eyes. He had not let even one of his men die. It was satisfying to have filled so well the responsibilities of a commander.

During the refueling, Shindo gathered reports from his excited men. The results that emerged were amazing. Totalling the tally of each pilot the number of planes shot down came to twenty-seven. Shindo himself had seen ten Chinese planes shot down. Among his men, there was one who had chased an enemy plane until it had crashed into the side of a mountain. Another had machine-gunned two planes on the ground at the Baishiyei airfield. Both had burned. These results appeared miraculous, but Shindo tended to think them natural. After all, they had gotten in the first blow from a good position, flying a fighter with a great superiority in speed over the I-15s and I-16s.

Only one plane had been damaged. The Zero of Oki, a petty officer second class, had been hit in a gasoline tank. The damage, however, was judged not serious enough to prevent him flying to Hankow.

There were tears in the eyes of the ground crew of the Ichang Airfield when they learned of these results. The mountains were close to the Ichang Airfield and many times the enemy had attacked from them. The ground crews guarding the airfield as a front line base suffered many hardships.

Meanwhile, the results of the air battle were telegraphed to Hankow Air Base from Ichang. Then the squadron took off for Hankow. At Hankow, the sky was dyed gorgeously by the sunset. At the airfield Rear Admiral Takijiro Onishi, commander of the Second United Air Corps, waited to greet the squadron along with several hundred people.

A shout rose: "Here they come!" All eyes concentrated in one direction at once. By a ridge of cumulonimbus cloud made luminous by the evening sun, points like crystals of sunshine appeared. The spot-like objects quickly increased in number and slowly began to come lower. Landing gears came out gracefully from the planes' undersides and one by one, thirteen Zero fighters landed on the runway.

Ground crews raced toward them. They surrounded each plane and guided it to its regular position. Lieutenant Shindo and other pilots came down from the planes and were instantly surrounded by people.

Shindo gathered his men around him and again had them report. Then he lined them up and waited for Captain Kiichi Hasegawa, the commandant of the air group.

"This is the general report of the combat," Shindo said calmly. Then he described the squadron's return to Chungking after the raid, the discovery of the twenty-seven Chinese fighters and the air combat. Finally he said: "We have for certain shot down, burned, or destroyed twenty-seven of the enemy fighters, consisting of I-15s and I-16s. All of our planes have just returned."

The group of people surrounding the pilots stirred. And when Shindo and his pilots began to walk in file toward Rear Admiral Onishi's tent, the people crowded round them came along, surrounding them closely.

Standing in a row beside Onishi in his tent were Commandant Hasegawa, Lieutenant Commander Kennosuke Tokinaga, the flight officer, Lieutenant Mikuma Minowa, group commander of the Twelfth Air Corps, and Shindo's fellow fighter squadron leaders, Lieutenant Tamotsu Yokoyama and Lieutenant Toshitaka Ito.

Shindo gave an outline of each pilot's performance in the combat to Rear Admiral Onishi. The pilot who had shot down the most planes was Warrant Officer Koshiro Yamashita. He had definitely shot down five aircraft. Petty Officer Second Class Oki, who had been hit in a gasoline tank, chased an I-15 even as he was choking over the fumes of the spilling gas, and shot it down. And Kitabatake and Yoneda, both petty officers, had destroyed two fighters that had escaped and landed at the Baishiyei Airfield.

Onishi listened, nodding to every word. When the report was finished, he looked at the thirteen pilots standing in a row before him.

"Just marvelous!" he said in a high-pitched voice. "Flying a new fighter, in the first air battle and against fighters superior in number, all the enemy were destroyed—this is a deed to be highly praised. This is the fruit of your effort. Thank you, men." Then a cup was given to each and a toast made with sake.

Yokoyama grasped Shindo's shoulder. As a colleague who had transported those same Zero fighters from Japan, he felt a deeply emotional bond at the miraculous outcome of the battle. Shindo and the others, joined by Yokoyama, talked about the Zero's performance in combat.

The one thing everyone mentioned was that the aircraft's speed seemed excessive. Pilots had felt as if they were falling forward or were unable to avoid overrunning the enemy fighters. But then, the I-15s and I-16s were so slow by comparison, that couldn't be helped. No one had any complaint about the Zero's dogfighting ability. It was almost the same as the Type 96 carrier-borne fighter's. The tremendous power of the twenty-millimeter cannon was a major topic. Many cases were reported of the wings of enemy aircraft shattering from the impact of the big bullets.

There was a case of one aircraft's retractable gear coming out during the battle, but it caused no trouble to the fighter at high speed. Another fighter had been unable to detach its drop tank as the squadron had been maneuvering into position for the attack and had been forced to go in with it still attached. But the tank also had not affected the plane's battle performance. One pilot even said: "I even wondered why the enemy planes went down so easily."

The sun had set. But the cheerful atmosphere at Hankow Air Base showed no sign of settling down.

Ten

The results of the Zero fighter's first campaign were reported immediately to Japan. They caused a sensation.

On September 14, the next day, the Naval Information Center of the Imperial General Headquarters made a special announcement that:

> On the fourteenth Kondo, the second in command of the Naval General Staff, and Toyota, the vice minister of the navy, sent a congratulatory telegram with the following message: "To Shimada, the Commander in Chief of the Fleet in the Chinese Theater. We congratulate you on cleverly trapping the remaining enemy fighters and destroying them."

And at the end of the next month, the following citation was sent to Shindo's squadron:

> To the fighter squadron of the Twelfth Air Corps under the command of Lieutenant Shindo:
>
> On the thirteenth of September 1940, you escorted bombers on an air raid on Chungking flying long-range over the mountain region of Szechwan. After out-maneuvering the enemy and tricking

them, you returned to Chungking again. You discovered and caught the enemy fighters with the cooperation of a land-based reconnaissance plane. Then, as confirmed, you shot down all of them, fighting bravely. This is a military action worthy of high praise.

For this you are awarded a citation.

[signed] The Commander in Chief of the China Theater Fleet, Shigetaro Shimada.

October 30, 1940

The results of the air combat were printed in the Japanese morning newspapers on September 15, two days after the battle. In the newspapers, the Hankow base was identified only as XX base, and the number of navy fighters engaged was not mentioned. And of course the stories omitted that these fighters were Zeros, designed and produced by Mitsubishi.

But those who worked on the design or manufacture of the Zero fighter at the Nagoya Aircraft Works immediately suspected that the fighter mentioned in the papers was the Zero. Only the Zero could have had the range to escort the bombers to Chungking. They also knew that fifteen Zeros had been transported to the continent. There was a lot of excitement. All concerned with the Zero knew how hard they had struggled to make the plane in the face of the navy's severe requirements and threats of change to the design. Then there had been the midair disintegration of the number two prototype and the complaints of some pilots that the plane was bigger than the Type 96 carrier-borne fighter that they liked so much. Now, however, the Zero had been in combat, the only test that counted, and it had emerged from that superbly. The aircraft's ability to make a nonstop flight from Hankow to Chungking, make a return to that city from fifty kilometers away, and yet still have fuel enough for an intense battle and flight to Ichang Airfield proved that it had a range far beyond any other fighter in the world. And to that triumph of design had been added the annihilating victory over the twenty-seven Chinese fighters, a demonstration of the Zero's superlative speed, dogfighting capability, and striking power. The designers and makers of the Zero could be proud; the navy's requirements had been more than satisfied.

But amid the joyous atmosphere at the works at the news of the Chungking victory, Horikoshi sat alone and silent at his desk. His face was blank except for all the tiredness that had emerged with the release of his tensions at last.

When later the navy finally told the Nagoya people that it actually had been thirteen of their Zeros in the Chungking engagement, and that all had returned safely and virtually unscathed from the amazing two-to-one fight, the excitement erupted all over again at the works.

In the navy, too, of course, the delight was great. All complaints about the Zero melted away. They acknowledged that Mitsubishi had met their requirements. So great was the navy's pleasure that Naval Aeronautical Headquarters decided to give certificates of commendation to Mitsubishi and Nakajima, the companies chiefly concerned with manufacturing the Zero. These two companies, it was decided, would also manufacture the plane in the future. Mitsubishi would be in charge of modifications.

For the Chinese air force, meanwhile, Chungking was a crushing defeat, both materially and morally. The air force had already been forced into retreat by the Type 96 carrier-borne fighter. Now the Chinese could hardly accept that all of their Polikparov I-15s and I-16s in the engagement, planes that were the pride of the Soviet aviation industry, had been quickly massacred by yet another new Japanese fighter. Even more humiliating, the defeat had taken place right over the capital, Chungking. The air force retreated to the area around Chengtu in remote Szechwan, far back from the front. There they tried to rebuild again.

One day Lieutenant Tamotsu Yokoyama got an unexpected order from Rear Admiral Takijiro Onishi. He was to fly alone to Chungking and make a low-altitude assessment of damage from the bombing.

The bombing of Chungking had been repeated tens of dozens of times, but damage to western China's biggest commercial center could only be assessed from aerial photographs. The real situation was not clear. That was why Onishi wanted Yokoyama to look over the town with his own eyes. There was also information that the main Chinese air force had retreated to Chengtu. But fighters might still secretly remain in the area. That would make it very dangerous for a single plane to fly over Chungking.

Yokoyama, however, accepted the order and the next day took off from Hankow base. Keeping unobtrusively to a high altitude, he flew the 405 nautical miles to Chungking and suddenly came down low only when he was near the town. Then he rushed the town at an altitude of 100 meters. In an instant he was jinking through a heavy hail of antiaircraft fire from the town's guns and machine guns. But the guns failed to hit a plane moving so low and fast. Keeping a sharp eye out for enemy fighters above, Yokoyama surveyed the town.

It was a miserable sight. The great town at the junction of the Kialing and Yangtze rivers had become a ruin of tiles and pebbles. Yokoyama thought the inhabitants must be hiding in caves dug into the mountainside, for there was no sign of people in the town. Checking the joint English-American settlement across the river, Yokoyama could see no trace of bombs having fallen there, and indeed, the inhabitants were outside their homes watching him go over without any sign of fear. That indicated that the land-based torpedo bombers were bombing accurately, hitting only the Chinese city of Chungking.

Yokoyama judged that he had seen enough and returned safely to Hankow. He reported to Rear Admiral Onishi that the city of Chungking had been completely destroyed and that it would be useless to bomb it any longer. As a result, air operations against the city were suspended. Instead, bombers were to begin flying farther west beyond Chungking to Chengtu, capital of Szechwan province. It was here the Chinese air force was trying to reconstitute itself.

The first attack on Chengtu was planned for October 4, 1940. The previous day, Lieutenant Yokoyama gathered his men for a meeting on tactics. He reiterated that the purpose of the fighters in air combat was to destroy both the enemy's planes and their skilled pilots. Although it wouldn't kill the pilots, enemy planes could be destroyed by attacking them on the airfield. That wasn't so easy as it looked, however. Planes on the ground usually had had their fuel extracted, so more than gunfire was needed to set them alight. Yokoyama went on to say that in case the Zeros did not encounter the enemy in the air, they were going to boldly attack the airfields instead.

Next day, Yokoyama and Sublieutenant j.g. Shirane led eight Zero fighters off Hankow base at 8:30 A.M. They were escorting twenty-seven torpedo bombers of the Thirteenth Air Corps. They landed at Ichang base, half way to Chungking, and refueled. Then they resumed the journey for distant Chengtu, 400 nautical miles to the west. From late fall to winter, the weather of Szechwan province was extremely bad. The Japanese raiding force encountered thick clouds. The ceiling was below 3,000 meters, concealing the ground from the airmen. The planes flew above the cloud. After a time, white, shining mountain ridges came into view on the left. They reached Chengtu at 2:10 P.M.

The torpedo bombers began attacking military facilities that had been identified by a reconnaissance plane earlier. The squadron of Zeros began a search for the enemy fighters. Pilot Hagiri, a flying petty officer first class, came upon a barrel-bodied I-16 and shot it down immediately. With the appearance of this single enemy fighter, Yokoyama thought that others would turn up. But they did not. Yokoyama decided then to attack the airfields.

The Zeros quickly went to Wenchiang Airfield, but found no planes on the ground. They went on to Taipingsi Airfield. From an altitude of 150 meters, Yokoyama made a survey and discovered more than thirty Chinese fighters skillfully concealed in side pockets. The day before, everyone had been briefed on his tactics for attacking planes on the ground. Now Yokoyama gave the signal to four pilots who were to operate in a predetermined group. Their planes boldly headed for the runway, one by one.

Flying Petty Officer Second Class Oishi was first to land. He was followed by Nakase, Hagiri, and Higashiyama. The four pilots jumped out of their planes and ran for the enemy aircraft, each man carrying a revolver, matches, and a piece of rag. At once machine guns in pillboxes round the field opened fire. The pilots tried to move forward, but as the firing from all sides grew more intense, they were pinned down. Yokoyama's other Zeros strafed the pillboxes, but the thick walls were not affected. That forced the pilots to give up. They ran for their planes before it was too late, and all managed to take off safely.

After that Yokoyama was forced to try repeated strafing attacks. The enemy planes were being destroyed one by one in this way when a Soviet-made Type SB bomber suddenly appeared and made ready to land. How it could be doing this when burning aircraft plainly showed the airfield was under attack could only be put down to some sort of delusion on the pilot's part. At 500 meters, the Zeros closed in. The engine was struck by twenty-millimeter cannon bullets and caught fire. The hapless bomber pulled up its nose, but in the next instant the nose dropped and the plane went into the ground and exploded. At about the same time, Hagiri came upon a formation of three I-16s and downed two.

Yokoyama gathered his men, and after confirming that they had suffered no losses, the Zeros left Chengtu and its sky broken by flames and pillars of black smoke.

The results of that attack were six aircraft shot down, including the SB medium bomber, and twenty-nine planes destroyed on the ground. Shigetaro Shimada, the commander in chief of the China Theater Fleet, awarded a citation to Yokoyama's squadron.

After that, the squadrons of Zero fighters flew to Chengtu, Chungking, and Kunming to attack Chinese fighters, with amazing results. From the first strike on August 19 against Chungking to the end on December 22 the planes made twenty-two sorties, and shot down fifty-nine Chinese fighters (including one unconfirmed kill) and damaged 101—without losing one Zero. These were unbelievable figures, and the Japanese navy went mad with joy at them.

Meanwhile, however, the international situation was worsening rapidly. In September 1940, Japan had occupied northern French Indochina in an attempt to cut off the supply route through that area by which the Chinese were receiving munitions. A few days after that, Japan's membership in the triple alliance with Germany and Italy forced Japan into a position of confrontation with the United States and England.

On September 26, the United States announced an immediate prohibition on the export of steel and iron scrap to Japan. England also announced that it would resume supplying the Chinese government with materials through Burma. To Japan, poor in natural resources, the embargo on exports put her under serious economic pressure. The reopening of the Burma supply route also made it certain the war with China would become more difficult to end.

By the end of 1940, Nagoya Aircraft Works had produced 120 Zero fighters and delivered them to the Japanese navy.

Eleven

On January 1941 (Showa 16) an event was held that greatly strengthened the navy's confidence in the Zero fighter. It was the annual fighter contest between the army and the navy.

This contest had been held several times before 1941 for the purpose of assessing the progress of fighters used by the army and navy. Both sides sent their representative fighters with veteran pilots. Before the contest, each side informed the other of the performance figures of its fighters. In addition, the published performances of first class foreign fighters such as the British Hurricane and Spitfire, and America's P-37 and P-38 were also given out.

The army had sent three fighters to the 1941 contest. The Ki-44 (later adopted as the Type 2 fighter, code name: Tojo), the Ki-43 (later adopted as the Type 1 fighter, code name: Oscar) and the Ki-27, a modified Type 97 fighter. The navy submitted only one plane, the Zero.

Flying for the navy were Lieutenant Yoshitomi, chief of the fighter squadron of the Yokosuka Naval Air Corps, Lieutenant Manbei Shimokawa, a squadron leader, and others. The army's pilots were chosen from men from the Aeronautical Technical Institute and the Akeno Flying School.

At the contest, each fighter competed in every type of performance. The results of the contest showed clearly the general superiority of the Zero.

On February 12, Jiro Horikoshi went to the Aeronautical Technical Establishment and discussed the results of the contest with Lieutenant Shimokawa and Lieutenant Kofukuda. At first, the army's Ki-43 fighter, powered by a Sakae engine that increased its output by fifty horsepower, compared to the Zero's Sakae 12 engine, had had a big advantage in payload, total weight, wing loading, weight per horsepower loading, and wingspan loading. Nevertheless, the Zero had dominated the Ki-43 in dogfighting. Horikoshi and the pilots suspected that this was because of the Zero's superior maneuverability and stability near stalling speed, the refined touch that the pilot could have in going from high speed to low, and the smaller air resistance of the plane. Yet judging from the statistics, it should have been impossible for the Zero to be superior to the Ki-43. The final proof that it was superior lay in the fact that the Ki-43 had been given a constant-speed propeller. This proved that its inferiority in dogfighting was due to the airframe design, not the propeller.

The Ki-44 was as inferior to the Zero in air combat as its statistics had suggested. It had been thought that the Ki-44 had a maximum speed of 550 kilometers per hour, much faster than the Zero. But in a comparison test, it was not faster than the Zero's 530 kilometers per hour. The Ki-44 was superior in the constant climb because of its much better weight per horsepower loading. But it was inferior in the other test events.

The modified Type 97 was highly valued for its dogfighting ability, and in dogfighting on a horizontal plane, it had certainly proved better. But at free dogfighting the Zero won, and in the other events it also proved superior.

It did not join in the contest, but among the foreign fighters, the Heinkel He-100, purchased by the navy, drew special notice because of its high speed. The plane was an experimental fighter made by the Heinkel Company. Its only purpose was high-speed interception. In its own tests the navy had recorded a speed for this aircraft of 650 kilometers per hour. It was definitely a plane of very advanced technology. It had a radical design that used most of the wing surface as a steam condenser for the steam cooled engine. But the He-100 had some bad defects. The engine would stop within a few minutes if hit by even a single bullet, and its lateral stability, maneuverability, and dogfighting ability were so poor that one wondered why it had been produced. It also had a very short range, since it had been designed purely to intercept bombers. Even if used to fly only at night against bombers, the He-100 was not practical.

The conclusion Horikoshi came to with Shimokawa and Kofukuda was that there was nothing more to add to the stability and the maneuverability of the Zero fighter. The published statistics of foreign planes appeared to overstate their capabilities by 10 percent. There also appeared to be a difference in standards between the army and the navy in judging performances.

The Zero's excellent performance at the army-navy fighter contest and its magnificent record in the air war in China now established the Zero as the proudest new fighter in the navy. Continuing operational tests after the contest proved that it had in every way achieved the impossible requirements set by the navy.

As it entered 1941, the Zero exhibited its prowess freely in China. On March 24 Yokoyama's squadron took part in a great air battle that showed off the Zero's fighting abilities particularly well.

Yokoyama had left Hankow with eight Zeros that day, and headed for Chengtu. According to information from a reconnaissance plane, the Chinese air force in Chengtu had been strengthened to more than thirty fighters for the defense of Chengtu. Yokoyama had decided to take the initiative, and though outnumbered by more than three to one, he set off to pounce on the Chinese while they were still making preparations for a battle. But when the Zeros reached Chengtu, no Chinese fighters could be found. They flew in a great circle, watching. But still none were sighted. The Zeros then dropped altitude quickly and approached the airfield. There they found seven Chinese fighters hidden in side pockets. Yokoyama's planes began to strafe these at once. One by one the planes caught fire. The Japanese were so occupied at this that they only noticed the arrival of some thirty I-15s and I-16s when the Chinese rushed in to attack.

The Chinese had succeeded in catching the Zeros at a serious disadvantage. But with their superior speed, the Japanese were able to dodge the first rush of their enemies, make a turn, reorganize and then themselves charge. A furious battle followed, but after only ten minutes, only Zeros were left flying above Chengtu. Twenty of the Chinese fighters (though of these three were unconfirmed) had been shot down. Yokoyama collected his men and headed back to Hankow.

The results of this combat made the value of the Zero all the more decisive. Flown by pilots whose skills outmatched their enemies', the Zero even began to seem mysterious—and not just to the horrified Chinese. The Chinese air force purchased fighters from the United States, Russia, Italy, England, and other countries, and was advised by groups of advisers from these countries. The Russians and Americans had even formed an air corps consisting of Russians and Americans.

Among them was Claire Lee Chennault, a retired flight captain of the U.S. Army Air Force. Chiang Kai-shek had great confidence in him as the able director of the Chinese air force and a determined foe of the Japanese air force. Chennault had originally been a fighter pilot and had his own theories about aerial combat, theories he strove to get the Chinese to accept. And for a time after the outbreak of war with Japan in July 1937, the skills and tactics of the Chinese air force introduced by Chennault caused the Japanese bombers heavy losses. But the Type 96 carrier-borne fighter, superior to all the foreign fighters on which the Chinese relied, decisively regained command of the air for Japan. The Chinese air force followed Chennault's advice and bought more foreign planes, and tried to rebuild itself. But then the Zero appeared.

Chennault was very alarmed to see a fighter even better than the unbeaten Type 96 carrier-borne fighter shooting down the best pilots of an air force he had been at such pains to rebuild. He reported what he knew of the Zero at once to the United States and England.

His objective evaluation predicted disaster for the Americans and British, confident as the world's most advanced nations aeronautically, if they tried fighting against the new Japanese naval fighter. But the Americans and British did not respond to this warning. They were certain that until only a few years ago Japanese aeronautical technology had depended on foreign technology, and they could not believe Japan was other than undeveloped still. It wasn't credible to them that Japan could design and build the new fighter Chennault was reporting. And it was beyond their imagination that the Type 96 carrier-borne fighter developed four years before the Zero had at that time already been above the standard of all other carrier-borne fighters in the world. At the time the Type 96 had been adopted, the Americans were using the German F3F fabric-covered fighter on their carriers.

The Chennault report was interpreted as an illusion, or a fake, and it was said that even if the results of the battle he reported were real, the Chinese losses were the consequence of the unskillfulness of their pilots.

The disbelief with which America and England greeted the Chennault report proved a great favor to the Japanese navy. The navy could now battle test the Zero fighter in China while remaining unnoticed by foreign countries.

Taking advantage of its long range, the Zero took part in all the war zones of China. On May 22, 1941, for the first time a Zero fighter, piloted by Flying Petty Officer Kimura, was shot down. A second was shot down a month later, on June 23. They were downed by heavy ground fire from Chinese troops. These were the only Zeros downed before the beginning of the Pacific War.

On August 31, 1941, the participation of Zeros in the Sino-Japanese War was suspended. The Japanese had achieved complete air superiority over China. The damage inflicted by the Zero on the Chinese air force in the one year since its introduction to the continent had been tremendous. One hundred sixty-two Chinese planes had been shot down (three were unconfirmed), and 264 had been destroyed for the loss of only two Zeros.

It was usual for planes to be modified to improve their performance or practicality after they had been accepted as fit and practical for use. In the case of the Zero, after the number one and two prototypes had been built as the 12Si carrier-borne fighter, the engine was changed from the Zuisei to the Sakae-12. With this engine the fighter had been adopted as the Type Zero carrier-borne fighter Model II. Mitsubishi produced sixty-four of these.

Then the Model II was improved. The total width of the Model II was twelve meters. This barely fit the elevator of an aircraft carrier. In an emergency, this was inconvenient, because in hoisting up and down there was a danger the wing tips would be broken. A shorter total width was also desirable for the purposes of storage on the aircraft carrier. In response, the width was modified so that fifty centimeters of both wing ends could be folded ninety degrees upward. This type of Zero was called Type Zero Model 21 and produced in large numbers.

However, even the amazing performance of this plane left room for complaints by navy pilots. These maintained that at a meter speed of about 300 kilometers per hour, the ailerons became heavy. They also said that at a meter speed of 370 kilometers per hour the ailerons were too heavy to make a slow roll without difficulty. At 240 kilometers per hour, however, the ailerons were light and easy in a slow roll. This same aileron complaint had also been made about the Type 96 fighter at the time of the test flights of its number one prototype. The problem had since been corrected, but with the same complaint appearing again, it was decided to make a study and actively measure the phenomenon.

Lieutenant Takayama of the airframe division of the Naval Aeronautical Technical Establishment came up with the solution. At the rear edges of the ailerons he fitted balance tabs that became effective after the landing gear was retracted. These made the ailerons easy to operate even at high speed. All Zeros after number 61 were fitted with these.

The confidence of the navy in the Zero was ever-increasing and its production was going smoothly. Mitsubishi had submitted 182 Zeros to the navy by the end of March 1941. At the Nakajima Aircraft Company Works, tooling up for Zero production was also going well.

Meanwhile, the international situation was getting more and more complex, and diplomatic negotiations between nations increasingly bewildering. Japan appointed a new ambassador, Nomura, to the United States to try to improve relations and start new negotiations. But on the other hand, Japan sent Matsuoka, the Minister of Foreign Affairs, to Europe and strengthened its relationship with Germany and Italy. Japan also concluded a treaty of neutrality with Russia.

In this situation, the Japanese Naval Corps went on with hard flight training every day. Then on April 16, an unusual accident occurred to the Zero number 140 flown by Lieutenant j.g. Yasushi Nikaido, the fighter squadron leader of the aircraft carrier *Kaga*. On that day, Nikaido took off at 3:15 P.M. to do special flights. Flying Zero number 140, he made left and right vertical turns, loops, slow rolls, and inverted flights. It was when he made a dazzling vertical turn that he noticed that wrinkles of a more marked nature than he had known before appeared on the surface plates of the left wing. On the right wing the wrinkles were minor. He also noticed that many wrinkles again appeared on the left wing when he tried a spectacular loop at the high speed of 480 kilometers per hour. Then, at about 3:30, he tried a deep dive from an altitude of 3,500 meters at an angle of about fifty degrees. From the altitude of 2,000 meters and at a meter speed of 540 kilometers per hour he tried another dive. Again wrinkles appeared on the left wing in many directions and the surface plates became loose.

Nikaido became alarmed and tried to pull up. But when the plane reached a speed of 550 kilometers per hour and 2,300 rpm, the plane suddenly developed vibrations so severe Nikaido's vision went white, and he almost lost consciousness. When he recovered he was relieved to find himself flying nearly horizontal. But to his surprise, both the right and left ailerons were lost and part of the surface of the upper wing ripped away. The pitot tube to measure speed was broken from its base and the hand of the speedometer stopped at 296 kilometers per hour.

Fortunately, Nikaido was close to the Kisarazu Airfield. He made a skillful emergency landing. The accident was reported to Naval Aeronautical Headquarters, the Naval Aeronautical Technical Establishment, and the Yokosuka Air Corps. The fighter squadron at Yokosuka also received an official report from the captain of the *Kaga*. Its leader, Lieutenant Manbei Shimokawa, immediately took it into his own hands to investigate.

Among those in the navy concerned with the Zero, the devotion of Shimokawa to the plane was exceptional. As a pilot with an inquiring mind and excellent flying skills, he had been deeply involved in evaluating the Zero in its development stages as the 12Si fighter. He had been an important supporter against the fighter's detractors and showed how great was his commitment when he personally made the test flights investigating the mid-air disintegration of the number two prototype. Shimokawa had also taken pilots from his own group for the squadron Yokoyama had taken to China. And after the success of the army-navy fighter contest in January 1941, it was Shimokawa with whom Horikoshi had sat down to discuss and celebrate the results. So deep, in fact, was Shimokawa's interest in the fighter that he felt something like a personal responsibility for the accident that had occurred to Nikaido's aircraft. That was why on the day after the accident, April 17, Shimokawa started his own enquiry.

In the hangar of the Yokosuka Naval Air Corps there were two Zero fighters. One, number 50, was without balance tabs. The other, number 135, Model 21, had balance tabs. Number 135 had once been assigned to the carrier *Akagi,* but had been returned because the aircraft had developed many wrinkles on the wing, wrinkles like those that had appeared on Nikaido's Zero. Shimokawa decided to test fly both aircraft to make a comparison.

On the morning of April 17 Shimokawa climbed into the cockpit of number 50 and took off. He took the aircraft up to 3,800 meters and began a deep dive at an angle of about fifty degrees. When his speedometer read 590 kilometers per hour, he began to pull up and came to horizontal flight at 1,200 meters. He carefully watched for wrinkling of the outer plates of the wings. But the few that appeared were not a cause for concern.

Shimokawa next took up number 135, the Zero with balance tabs and that had developed bad wrinkles. He climbed to 4,000 meters, and repeated the deep dive he had made with number 50. At about 2,000 meters he started to pull up and was flying level at 1,500 meters.

That deep dive test went well. Shimokawa climbed again and started a second dive. At 1,500 meters he began to pull up. It was then that observers saw what appeared to be a big white paper fly away from the left wing. Something black leaped out also. Number 135 turned left twice, seemed to recover. Then suddenly the aircraft dropped it nose and dove into the sea in ten fathoms of water about 300 meters off Natsu Island.

Shouts rose from the airfield. They all hoped Lieutenant Shimokawa had bailed out. But no parachute was seen to open in the sky. Immediately an effort to recover the plane got underway. Rescuers found Shimokawa inside, his head entirely crushed into the instrument panel. At news of the popular Shimokawa's death, everyone from his superior officers to subordinates cried. His body was carried into the corps building.

Horikoshi, told the same day of the accident, was deeply shocked. Everyone at the Nagoya works concerned with the plane knew of Shimokawa's devotion. His powerful backing had been important to the plane's acceptance by the navy. It seemed especially tragic that he had been killed undertaking, of his own initiative, such a daring test flight to discover the cause of Nikaido's accident.

Next day Horikoshi went to the Naval Aeronautical Establishment at Yokosuka for Shimokawa's funeral. He could not help sobbing when he saw Shimokawa's photograph in front of the altar. Shimokawa had always been gentle and warm with Horikoshi and a source of pointed advice.

To investigate the accident, a committee was set up within the Aeronautical Technical Establishment. They began by looking at the condition of the plane. The engine was heavily damaged, but the twisted propeller was still attached. The airframe was bent out of its original shape and part of the mainspar had become fused with the fuselage. Ailerons and horizontal stabilizers had been torn out and could not be found. Eyewitnesses confirmed, however, that number 135 had been almost intact when it had struck the sea, quite different from the crash of the number two prototype, which had disintegrated in midair.

It was noticed that both the number 140 plane flown by Lieutenant j.g. Nikaido and Shimokawa's number 135 Zero had balance tabs. This might have something to do with the accident. For the time being, the Aeronautical Technical Establishment restricted the maximum speed of Zeros with balance tabs to an instrument speed of 460 kilometers per hour and limited pilots to pulling up below 5gs. Flights practicing especially violent maneuvers were prohibited also, though not for planes without balance tabs.

Meanwhile, the investigation into the accident found many points to consider. Those planes without balance tabs had been tested enough times to confirm that they had the strength to withstand powerful vibration and static force. The wrinkles that appeared on the surface plates of their wings were few. Planes with the balance tabs had had frequent air combat tests, but deep diving tests had not been carried out.

The Aeronautical Establishment reflected on this omission. Engineer Yasushi Matsudaira commenced wind tunnel tests to reexamine flutter. As a result, suspicion fell on the flutter tendencies of the aileron. The critical speed set by Mitsubishi for aileron rotational wing compound flutter had depended on vibration tests of the real plane and wind tunnel tests using the model wing of two years before. That speed was set at 926 kilometers per hour. Matsudaira's tests now revealed, however, that flutter might unexpectedly occur at 600 kilometers per hour.

In the wing models Matsudaira had used in his wind tunnel tests, the distribution of torsion bending stiffness and mass were exactly proportional to the measured results of the real plane in this type of wind tunnel test. But when he compared the results of his flutter tests with vibration tests of the real plane, Matsudaira discovered the cause of the accident. In making this discovery, a basic flaw was revealed in the testing process for flutter that had been used at the development stage of the Zero and all other aircraft up till then. This was that the flutter models used exactly copied the shape and nearly exactly the mass distribution of the real plane. But such models had not simulated the stiffness distribution.

Engineer Matsudaira's study increased at a bound Japan's knowledge of flutter and contributed much to the design of its fast aircraft. The Zero and other high-speed aircraft were retested for vibration, and had their flutter models remade and retested. Flutter speeds were recalculated, and as a result, the maximum speeds for the Zero and other aircraft were reduced considerably.

A question remained about one thing. The findings had shown that flutter in the Zero occurred at almost the same speed whether the ailerons had balance tabs or not. The advantage of the balance was that it prevented the aileron from becoming too heavy at high speed. That made it easy to pull up from a deep dive using ailerons. Now, however, this was seen as a possible disadvantage. The easy use of the ailerons led to a tendency to maneuver the plane to the point at which wrinkling of the wings' surface plates became noticeable or even loose and their rigidity much lowered. For these reasons, pilots became suspicious of Zeros with balance tabs. Later, the tabs were abolished.

A Japanese Zero in flight. Photo courtesy National Archives.

Japanese Zero fighters ready to take off for Pearl Harbor from an aircraft carrier. Photo courtesy National Archives.

Japanese Zeros and hangars at Aslito Airfield, Saipan. Photo courtesy National Archives.

Japanese Zero kamikaze closing in on the USS *Suwannee* near Leyte Gulf. Photo courtesy National Archives.

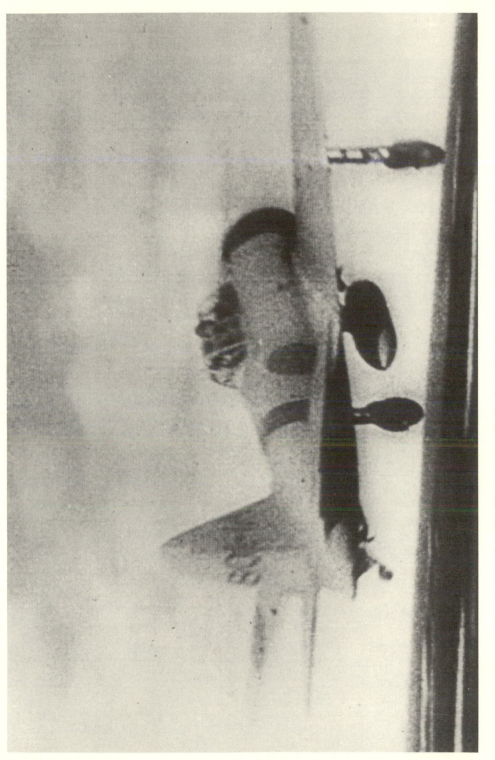

A Japanese Zero takes off from an aircraft carrier. Photo courtesy National Archives.

Twelve

On June 22, 1941, Germany declared war on Russia. An enormous force of 150 divisions (four million men) plunged into Soviet territory. England and the United States at once declared themselves in support of Russia, and the world became divided into two groups.

Just over a month later, on July 29, Japan began to occupy southern French Indochina, based upon the treaty for the mutual security of Japan and French Indochina. The aim was to shut off the supply of materials to Chungking and at the same time to secure raw materials from the area. The United States, however, judged this occupation a threat to the Netherlands East Indies and Singapore. The United States froze all Japanese assets. England and the Netherlands followed with a similar retaliation.

With its great dependence on the import of raw materials from the United States and the Netherlands, this economic rupture was very serious to Japan, more damaging than an attack by armed forces. Liquid fuel especially became critical. It was estimated that the country's private supplies would run out within the year if the embargo lasted. In an effort to ease the embargo, Japan tried hard to improve its relations with the United States. But anti-Japanese feeling was so strong it began to seem among the army and navy that war would be unavoidable.

In the grave mood surrounding military leaders, opinions in favor of war proliferated rapidly. Finally, they became the majority view. Japan was to dare to challenge the United States, England, and the Netherlands in spite of the risks, rather than wait to lose its power through economic oppression. Based on this view, it was decided at the Imperial Conference on September 6, 1941, to begin preparations for war without hesitation against England, the United States, and the Netherlands. Immediately the army and navy began serious preparations.

The Japanese government sent Samuro Kurusu as an ambassador extraordinary, to break the deadlock of negotiations with the United States and show Japan's conditions for making concessions. But the Americans offered no concessions on their side. This quickened the preparations of the army and navy for war.

The army planned a southern operation that would include landing on the Malay Peninsula with the aim of securing the resources of the South Sea area. The navy planned a surprise attack on the main American Pacific Fleet in Pearl Harbor. The planning was led by Admiral Isoroku Yamamoto, commander in chief of the combined fleet (this meant the entire Japanese naval offensive force. Originally it had meant the combined regular and reserve fleets). Based on these two large operations, the forces of the army and navy were re-formed and secretly transferred.

In a prolonged war against the United States it was obvious that Japan's lesser resources and industrial strength would strongly affect its military might. As long as the Pacific Ocean was the battlefield, Japan's navy would be the prime factor in deciding the war against America. Estimates of the ship-building capabilities of each nation showed, however, how great the industrial strength of the United States was. At the start of the war, the ratio of naval ship building would be 7.5 to ten in favor of the United States. By 1943, the Americans would be building ships at a rate of two for every one built by the Japanese. By 1944, that ratio would have become three to one.

The difference in the ratios for naval aircraft building was as great. Even in 1942, the Japanese had only 4,000 such aircraft compared to America's 48,000. The Japanese would be able to build 8,000 in 1943, but the Americans would be able to make 85,000. In 1944, the United States would make 100,000 against Japan's 10,000.

The Japanese navy was doomed, then, to fight America's greater industrial strength. Yet it was still expected to win. The navy decided winning was not impossible if the American Pacific Fleet was severely crippled at the start of the war and finally destroyed in a sea battle between battleship squadrons using Japan's better quality against America's quantity. However, there were many risks to consider.

It would be extremely difficult to win a naval battle at the beginning of the war, and their chances would diminish greatly if the war was prolonged. For these reasons, much was hoped of the negotiations with the United States, even though preparations for war were going ahead. However, the letter handed to the Japanese Government from the U.S. Secretary of War Cordell Hull decided the issue.

The Hull note was very severe. It asked for the evacuation of the Japanese army, navy, and air force and police from China and French Indochina and also for Japan's withdrawal from the Triple Alliance. From the Japanese point of view, such a proposal could only be considered a final note, lacking any spirit of compromise.

The headquarters of the Japanese army and navy now decisively determined to begin the war. At an Imperial conference on December 1, it was decided that the day to open hostilities would be December 8, 1941. The commanders of all military forces were informed.

The Japanese navy planned two major operations. One was to attack Pearl Harbor. The other was the Southern Operation, aiming at the destruction of all the fleets and air forces of their enemies in Asia. This operation would be in cooperation with the army's landing on the Malay Peninsula. Both operations were mainly air operations.

The naval air force available for these operations consisted of 519 fighters, 257 carrier-borne bombers, 510 carrier-borne torpedo bombers, 445 land-based torpedo bombers, and others. The whole force totaled 3,202.

Among the fighters, Zeros formed the majority. Of the 371 fighters directly assigned to the attack operations, 322 were Zeros and the remaining forty-nine were Type 96 carrier-borne fighters. In short, the Zero was to lead the Japanese navy's challenge against the fleets of England, the United States, and the Netherlands.

The Americans had a low opinion of the Japanese air force, both of its quality and quantity. Chennault's warnings about the Zero had been ignored entirely. The Americans believed that the Japanese aviation industry was small in scale and dependent entirely on foreign countries for designs and manufacturing technology. They believed that even when the Japanese built foreign planes under license, they could not build well enough to duplicate the original performances of such aircraft. They also thought Japanese pilots were inferior in skill. Indeed, the general view was that everything in Japan was inferior.

How the Zero would match up against the fighters of England and America was not known. Though the Zero had won overwhelming victories in China, it had never encountered the latest fighters of these nations. But the navy's trust in the Zero was absolute, and it showed in the number of Zeros assigned to the Pearl Harbor operation, and also to the Southern Operation.

The land-based air corps of the Eleventh Air Fleet, stationed at Formosa, southern Indochina, and Palau Island, under Vice Admiral Nishizo Tsukahara, was assigned for this operation. The air corps possessed 566 planes to be used in the drive south. Among them were 244 Zeros, manned by such excellent pilots as Commander Motoharu Okamoto, Commander Yasuno Kozono, Commander Takeo Shibata, Lieutenant Hideki Shingo, and Lieutenant Tamotsu Yokoyama.

In the Pearl Harbor attack, the most important mission belonged to the First Air Fleet, the nucleus of the Hawaii Strike Force, commanded by Vice Admiral Chuichi Nagumo. On November 16, the ships of the Hawaii Strike Force began leaving the Inland Sea of Japan in small groups or alone and gathered in desolate Hitokappu Bay on remote Etorofu Island in the southern Kuriles. The force of thirty ships sailed from the bay on November 26 at 6 P.M.

The Hawaii Strike Force, the main body of this operation, was divided into the first strike wave and the second strike wave. Each consisted of a horizontal bomber group, a torpedo bomber group, a dive bomber group, and a fighter group to dominate the air. The general commander of these groups, Commander Mitsuo Fuchida, was also to command the first strike wave. Lieutenant Commander Shimazaki was to command the second strike wave.

The fighter group, which was to advance before the rest of the strike wave and take control of the air above Pearl Harbor, consisted entirely of Zeros. Lieutenant Commander Shigeru Itaya led the forty-three Zeros of the first strike wave. Itaya had had a long association with the Zero, having been the one who presented it at the inspection of the first full scale wooden mockup of the 12Si fighter in April of 1938 and on other occasions. Leading the thirty-four Zeros of the second strike wave was Lieutenant Saburo Shindo, who had led the spectacular destruction of twenty-seven Soviet-made fighters above Chungking just over a year before in the Zero's first battle encounter with an enemy.

Though the task force sailed secretly toward Hawaii after departing Hitokappu bay, it was ready to turn back at a favorable turn of negotiations with the United States. However, on the night of December 2, 1941, the task force received a telegram in code from the commander in chief of the combined fleet:

"Climb Mt. Niitaka 1208."

To climb Mt. Niitaka (Mt. Niitaka, the present Mt. Chia-i of Taiwan, was in Japanese-occupied Formosa, and in 1941 the highest mountain in Japan's dominions) meant "Carry out the attack following the plan." "1208" indicated that the day for war to break out was December 8.

The nucleus of the Hawaii Strike Force was six aircraft carriers: *Akagi, Kaga, Soryu, Hiryu, Shokaku,* and *Zuikaku* (both *Shokaku* and *Zuikaku* were 29,800-ton twin sisters commissioned just a few months before. The attack on Pearl Harbor was actually a shakedown cruise for each). They were accompanied by two modern battleships, *Hiei* and *Kirishima,* escorted by the heavy cruisers *Tone* and *Chikuma.* Seven tankers, without which the operation would be impossible, brought up the rear: *Kyokuto Maru, Kenyo Maru, Kokuyo Maru, Shinkoku Maru, Nihon Maru, Toho Maru,* and *Toei Maru.* Screening and escorting of the task force was the responsibility of the cruiser *Abukuma,* leading nine of the newest and best destroyers in the navy: *Urakaze, Tanikaze, Hamakaze, Isokaze, Kasumi, Arare, Shiranui, Kagero,* and *Akigumo.* Far ahead of the fleet scouted the submarines *I-19, I-21,* and *I-23.*

North of Midway Island, on December 4, after fueling from the tankers at sea, the fleet turned southeast and approached Hawaii. The danger of being spotted by American patrol planes, submarines, or merchant ships during the approach to Hawaii posed a constant threat for the task force. The possibility of this was considered great enough that it had been determined that the fleet would turn back if spotted two days before the attack date. If it were seen the day before the strike was to be launched, the decision to turn back or not was to depend on the situation.

But the greatest concern was whether the American fleet was in harbor or not. Japanese intelligence agents, stationed in Hawaii for some time, had been sending precise reports on the movements of American vessels in and out of Pearl Harbor to the Naval Department of the Imperial General Headquarters. These reports were secretly relayed to the task force approaching Hawaii.

At 8:50 P.M. on December 7, only three hours before midnight of December 8, the date on which war would break out, the Naval Department sent a coded telegram to the task force:

> 1:   On December 6 [the seventh by Japanese time] the following ships are in port: nine battleships, three light cruisers, three seaplane carriers, seventeen destroyers, four light cruisers, three destroyers in dock. All the aircraft carriers and heavy cruisers are at sea.
>
> 2:   Nothing unusual has been found about the fleet. There is still no control of lights on Oahu Island.
>
> The Imperial General Headquarters is sure of your success.

The Task Force had not been expecting to find the American carriers gone to sea, but in spite of that, every ship of the task force was engulfed with joy. Six hundred miles north of Oahu the task force completed its final refueling, and dropped its last tankers. Now comprised only of the fighting ships, the fleet swung due south and increased speed to twenty knots. It was now that Vice Admiral Nagumo's flagship *Akagi* ran out the historic Z flag, which Admiral Togo had hoisted at the battle of Tsushima (when Japan defeated the Imperial Russian Fleet and took its place as a modern naval power in the world). Then it relayed the historic signal sent from Admiral Isoroku Yamamoto, commander in chief of the combined fleet: "The rise and fall of the Empire depends on this battle. Every man will do his duty."

This was the signal to complete preparations for battle in all ships. They were ready in no time. With sharp sounds from their catapults, the heavy cruisers *Tone* and *Chikuma* launched type Zero sea scout planes to make a reconnaissance of Pearl Harbor. On each of the aircraft carriers, the aircraft for the first strike wave, headed by the Zero fighters, finished last-minute checks and waited for take-off time.

At 1:30 A.M. the order came: "Start engines!" and at once the propellers of all the planes began to rotate. The aircraft carriers steered into the wind. The seas were high. As the ships pitched into them spray rose from the breaking waves of the dark sea and swept over the flight decks.

In the light of dawn, green signal lamps were waved violently in an arc. "Start launching!"

On the pitching decks, the roar of the engines increased. Zero fighters started to take off one by one from each carrier. Attack planes followed. Cheers rang out all over the ships, and caps and hands were waved vigorously as the whole first strike wave force of 183 planes rose one by one above the sea of oncoming waves.

The planes took up their formation led by Fuchida, the general commander, and after making a big circle, they turned for Oahu. Horizontal bombers, torpedo bombers, and dive bombers made orderly formations by groups. Above them, Zero fighters under the command of Lieutenant Commander Itaya flew close escort.

Those on the flight decks of the aircraft carriers kept on waving their caps to the figures of the great number of planes melting into a sky that was showing the color of dawn.

At the Nagoya Aircraft Works of Mitsubishi the use of oxcarts was becoming more and more frequent. The land-based torpedo bomber, an adaptation of the Zero fighter, had been officially adopted as the Type 1 land-based torpedo bomber six months before the Pearl Harbor attack. The navy had confidence in its long range, and at last determined to begin mass production.

At midnight, a chain of oxcarts, loaded with Type 1 land-based torpedo bombers, slowly started out on the long, bad road to Kagamigahara Airfield. The carts were loaded with either fuselages or wings, and these shook with every jolt of the carts. The breath of the oxen was white in the cold air.

It still took twenty-four hours to move aircraft the forty-eight kilometers to Kagamigahara by oxcart. On the day of the Pearl Harbor attack, oxcarts loaded with fuselages or wings, trundled clumsily along the rough country road.

Thirteen

Under the command of Lieutenant Commander Shigeru Itaya, forty-three Zero fighters flew toward Oahu Island. They were accompanied by the 140 Type 97 torpedo bombers (code name: Kate) or Type 99 dive bombers (code name: Val) of the first strike wave. The cloud was dense, and against their will, the aircraft had to climb to 3,000 meters to get above it. It was already dawn, and the shadowy black clouds began to shine white.

Commander Mitsuo Fuchida, the general commander of the first strike wave, was trying to detect the direction to Pearl Harbor by following the radio waves from the Honolulu radio station. The Honolulu station was loudly broadcasting leisurely jazz. That told Fuchida that the American navy in Hawaii was still unaware of the task force's approach.

Then the radio began broadcasting the weather. "Generally half-fine, mountains covered with clouds, cloud ceiling is 3,500 feet, visibility fine, north wind at ten knots."

Fuchida was pleased to find out precisely how the weather was in Hawaii. He instantly decided to depart from the planned route of his approach to Pearl Harbor. By the radio broadcast, the cloud ceiling was about 1,000 meters. The attack plan called for an approach to

Pearl Harbor from the northeast, crossing the mountains on the east side of Oahu Island. But following this course, the strike group would be at a disadvantage if by chance they encountered enemy fighters. Fuchida now judged that with the wind from the north, they should instead turn along the west side of the island and approach from the south.

Already an hour and thirty minutes had passed since they had taken off from the aircraft carriers. Oahu Island should be close. The Zero fighters watched the cloud closely, but saw no figures of planes other than the groups of Japanese aircraft they were escorting.

At 3:00 A.M. (7:30 A.M. Honolulu time) Fuchida located Kahuku Point, the northern tip of Oahu, through an accidental break in the cloud and ordered a turn to the right for all planes. Then, after ten minutes, he decided to order all the planes to deploy for attack.

He reached for his signal gun and fired a flare—the predetermined signal for the surprise attack if they had not been found by enemy planes. Had they been discovered, the signal was to be two flares.

The plan called for the following order of attack. First the torpedo bombers would go in, then the level bombers. The last assaulting wave would be the dive bombers. In case of an American attack, however, the order of attack was to be reversed. First the dive bombers would attack, then the level bombers, and finally the torpedo bombers, releasing their very efficient and powerful torpedos at the berthed warships in the shallow waters of Pearl Harbor.

Naturally, the Zero fighters were to lunge ahead of the attacking aircraft to clear the skies of enemy fighters. Lieutenant Commander Itaya's Zeros, however, were flying considerably higher than the attack groups and separated by cloud, they were not aware of Fuchida's signal. They remained in their orderly formation and did not change to an attack formation. Irritated, Fuchida fired another signal to get the Zeros' notice. It worked. The fighters acknowledged at last, and climbing high to their attack position, hastened toward Oahu.

But Takahashi, leader of the dive bombers, thought that this second flare meant that the attackers had been spotted by the Americans and that the second attack plan—the reverse of the first—was now to be followed. In the second plan, the dive bombers led the assault, instead of coming in last. Meanwhile, Lieutenant Commander Shigeharu Murata, the leader of the torpedo bomber group, correctly read the meaning of Fuchida's second flare and immediately began to lead his torpedo bombers to a lower altitude, indicating he would lead the attack according to the one-flare plan.

Through a break in the cloud Pearl Harbor began to be dimly visible ahead with the masts of the U.S. fleet anchored around Ford Island. Fuchida confirmed the presence of each ship calmly through his binoculars and at last, at 3:19 A.M., he sent to the first strike wave the signal "To, to, to, to. ..."—a chain of "to," meaning "All planes launch attack in full force." Three minutes later, Fuchida also signalled *Akagi:* "Tora, Tora, Tora"—the prearranged code signal for "We have succeeded in making a complete surprise attack." The message was instantly relayed to the Communication Section of the Imperial General Headquarters in Tokyo, far away.

Following the first plan for a complete surprise attack, Lieutenant Commander Murata's Type 97 torpedo bombers rapidly got onto the carefully planned courses necessary to torpedo the American ships. Now, however, trouble started for them. The dive bombers under Lieutenant Commander Takahashi, still under the impression from the second flare that they must attack first, had already gone in, and the spreading smoke and explosions of their bombs were making it difficult to see the American ships clearly. Realizing that visibility would rapidly get even worse, Murata hastened to take a short cut rather than the planned course to deployment. Guiding his wing men, he rushed at high speed into the bay.

From the underside of each bomber skimming the sea surface, a torpedo dropped away. Many white wakes ran on the water. The wakes ran straight into the sides of the American ships anchored in a regular pattern. In that instant, magnificent waterspouts rose high into the sky and glinted in the morning sun to the thunder of explosions.

Takahashi's fifty-one dive bombers had divided into two groups. Takahashi led the main group in a bombing attack on Ford Island and Hickam Field. Lieutenant Akira Sakamoto attacked Wheeler Airfield—air base of the American fighters. Both groups then attacked the Ewa and Kaneohe airfields.

Fuchida's level bombing group followed. Consisting entirely of Type 97 carrier-borne torpedo bombers, the planes attacked from 3,000 meters. Oahu Island was quickly covered with fire and smoke as black as a volcano's.

Lieutenant Itaya's Zeros circled Pearl Harbor at high speed, keeping an eye out for attackers. Only four U.S. fighters climbed up to defend the base. All were furiously attacked and shot down. It was the first contact the Zero had had with American fighters. With the sky empty of U.S. fighters, and fire from the ground growing more intense, the Zeros split up into six groups and went to strafe the military airfields with their twenty-millimeter cannon.

Pearl Harbor had by now turned into a ghastly sight. Many American naval ships were in a wretched state, blackened and blasted. Some were wrapped in huge flames, others were over on their sides, or capsized, or resting on the bottom of the shallow harbor. The water of the bay danced to a heavy rain of splinters or shook heavily with falling waterspouts. The merciless attack was not over, however. The white wakes of torpedos still coursed the water, and bombs kept falling with heavy explosions on ships and land facilities.

At last the first strike wave had spent its bombs and torpedos, and at 4:00 A.M. Fuchida ordered all the first strike wave to return to the carriers. Their success had been complete.

The second strike wave under Lieutenant Commander Shigekazu Shimazaki was already on its way in and had reached Kahuku Point. Its 167 aircraft were in attack formation. Shimazaki led the fifty-four level bombers, all Type 97 torpedo bombers. The seventy-eight Type 99 dive bombers were commanded by Lieutenant Commander Takashige Egusa. Lieutenant Saburo Shindo led the thirty-six Zero fighters.

Shimazaki ordered the second strike to begin at 4:25 A.M. By now, however, the antiaircraft fire from Pearl Harbor was very heavy. The area was covered in a pall of black smoke and great fires, and it was almost impossible to locate targets. For this reason, the level bombers reduced altitude to 1,800 or 1,500 meters from 3,000, even though they knew the power of their bombs would be reduced. Even so, they were faced with a most difficult prospect. With all the ships hidden in smoke, the pilots could not decide which to attack. Finally they decided that ships still firing up at them must be less damaged. The dive bombers followed the rising tracers down to these smoke shrouded targets.

Meanwhile, Shindo's Zeros rushed to take up their position above the attack groups. They found a few American fighters in the air, and shot them down. Then they attacked Kaneohe Field with their cannons.

As general commander of the strike waves, Fuchida had remained above Oahu while the first strike wave departed and the second came in. He took pictures to confirm results, and flew back with the second wave when it was finished.

On board the ships of the task force mad joy reigned at the success of the attack. It seemed nothing short of a miracle that the task force had escaped detection in the long voyage from the Kuriles and that the first strike wave, too, had escaped on the flight into Oahu. The results were also more than anyone had expected.

Many at headquarters now insisted that a third strike wave should be launched to take advantage of the victory. Hard discussions followed. It was thought that a third wave might have losses because the antiaircraft fire was becoming increasingly heavy. Finally, however, Vice Admiral Chuichi Nagumo, commander of the task force, decided that the purpose of the operation, to destroy the American fleet, had been achieved and he decided to turn back immediately. Recovery of the attack and reconnaissance planes began at once. Then the task force started to run north at high speed.

The surprise attack on Pearl Harbor had achieved results rare in naval history. Four American battleships, the *Arizona, West Virginia, California*, and *Oklahoma*, and the target ship *Utah* had been sunk. One battleship, the *Nevada*, had been badly damaged, along with two light cruisers, three destroyers, and one repair ship. The battleships *Maryland, Tennessee*, and *Pennsylvania* had also been badly damaged. The Americans had also lost 231 planes, shot down or burned on the ground. The main force of the American fleet had received a deadly blow.

Nagumo's force, on the other hand, had got off lightly. Five torpedo bombers, fifteen dive bombers and nine Zeros had failed to return. Among the pilot losses was the carrier *Soryu's* Zero squadron leader Lieutenant Fusata Iida, who had taken off with the second strike wave.

Iida's story was known. He had gathered his men before takeoff and instructed them that if it was impossible to return to the carrier, they should crash their aircraft and kill themselves to avoid capture. Iida had strafed Kaneohe Airfield with eight other Zeros. But his plane was hit. Gas started leaking. It seemed then he judged it impossible to return. After showing his subordinate the direction to the carrier, he suddenly turned back from his companions, waving a hand at them, and dove into the airfield.

At the same time as the first planes of Nagumo's Hawaii Strike Force were successfully attacking Pearl Harbor, Japan's armed forces were launching other attacks. In Formosa, two groups of Zeros were about to take off. At the Takao base, Lieutenant Tamotsu Yokoyama was leading fifty Zeros belonging to the Third Air Corps. At the Tainan base, thirty-four fighters of the Tainan Air Corps under Lieutenant Hideki Shingo were about ready to go.

While the navy had been most concerned with the execution of the Pearl Harbor attack, the army had been concentrating on its huge Southern Operation, a series of surprise landings on the Malay Peninsula, the Philippines and other areas. Air power was a major component of these attacks. For the Malay Peninsula landings, the army air force took charge of protecting the troopships. The navy's air force had charge of attacks in the Philippines, where the Americans had a force of planes that was almost equal in size to that of their Japanese attackers. Should these aircraft attack the Japanese troop convoys, heavy damage would result. The Japanese Naval Air Corps would have to attack first to neutralize this threat.

The American planes were stationed at Iba and Clark airfields in the vicinity of Manila on Luzon Island. Yokoyama would lead the attack on Iba, Shingo the attack on Clark Field. Each Zero force would be escorting fifty-four Type 96 land-based torpedo bombers or Type 1 land-based torpedo bombers.

The operation was only possible because of the amazing range of the Zero. It was about 450 nautical miles from Formosa (now Taiwan) to the American air bases in the Philippines. That was a distance even greater than the one from Hankow to Chungking. It was too long even for the Zero. For that reason, the plan was to use the aircraft carriers *Ryujo, Zuiho,* and the *Kasuga Maru,* a merchant ship converted to a carrier.

However, these carriers had problems. The first was their small size. *Ryujo,* 9,400 tons, could load only twenty-four planes compared to the forty-eight loaded by *Shokaku* and other large fleet carriers. The 11,200-ton *Zuiho* also only loaded twenty-four planes. At 17,000 tons *Kasuga Maru* was the biggest of the small carriers, but being a converted merchant ship she loaded even fewer aircraft—twenty-three. In total, only seventy-one Zeros could be loaded in these ships. But of that number, some were needed to protect the carriers from attacking aircraft. That made the number of planes left for the attack even smaller.

Their second problem was their speed. Normally, an aircraft carrier ran upwind at full speed to help its aircraft launch. These carriers were so slow, however, that if the wind was less than twenty miles an hour, the aircraft had to use the full deck length to get off. For this reason, only half the load of fighters could be stationed on the flight deck. This meant that after these had been launched, time had to be spent bringing the other half up from the hangar deck for launching. As a result the flight of aircraft would be divided in two groups from the start.

A more fundamental problem with the Philippines attack lay with the bomber groups. If they started from their bases in Formosa, could they join the fighters being launched at sea? The Japanese were well aware that the Americans and English in Malaya, the Philippines, and other locations would be intently watching for any action by approaching Japanese warships and monitoring their signals. If the Japanese were detected, they would be attacked first. This made it necessary for the three carriers to approach the Philippines in radio silence.

That, however, would make coordination with the bomber bases in Formosa impossible. Even a prearranged rendezvous would be impossible if anything such as bad weather or other conditions forced a change of time.

On the other hand, there remained strong opinions against a launch from aircraft carriers. Vice Admiral Nishizo Tsukahara, the commander in chief of the Eleventh Air Fleet, invited more discussion about the Zero's range with head officers of the air corps and experts at the Aeronautical Technical Establishment. An actual test of the fuel consumption rate was carried out by a Zero fighter group. As a result, it was confirmed at the end of October that it was possible for the Zeros to fly from Formosa to the Philippines if the cruising range of the engine was reduced from 1,850 rpm to 1,650–1,700 rpm and by changing the pitch of the propeller properly.

This news filled the bases with joy. On October 25, Tsukahara canceled the launch of the Zeros from the little carriers. On that same day, the first secret reconnaissance flight over British-held Batan Islands was tried.

The problem of the Zero's range had been solved for the moment. But a stepping stone was needed for supply and maintenance, as Ichang had served the Zeros on their return from the long Chungking flights. The Batan Islands were midpoint between Formosa and the Philippines and had a small airfield. It looked to be a favorable location, if it could be obtained.

Reconnaissance of Luzon Island and the airfields was necessary. However, the fear grew that if the reconnaissance was detected, the secret Japanese preparations for war might be revealed. Driven by the absolute necessity for information, the reconnaissance plane started flights on November 20. But with the date of the declaration of war drawing so close, fear of leaks caused the flights to be halted again on December 5. The resulting lack of information then began to cause great uneasiness among the operation's leaders, because to be effective, their attack was going to have be a surprise.

It had to be exactly timed, too. The minute Nagumo's task force struck Pearl Harbor, the American forces in the Philippines would be told of it. To achieve surprise, the Japanese had to be rushing the American airfields around Manila at almost the same time that Pearl Harbor was being attacked.

The time of the raid on Pearl Harbor was fixed at dawn on December 7 (Honolulu time). Since that would be midnight to 1 A.M. on December 8 in the Philippines, it was suggested that the bombers should start first and bomb in the night. The Zeros could follow them.

The results of night bombing would be small, however, so it was finally decided to allow the bombers and Zeros to reach Luzon as a group fifteen minutes after sunrise, at 6:15 A.M. on December 8. Launch time from Formosa would be 2:30 A.M.

On December 7, the Eleventh Air Fleet placed a curfew on all members, and told them for the first time that war against the United States, England, and the Netherlands would break out the next day. A tense atmosphere came over the Tainan and Takao bases. Meanwhile, with air reconnaissance canceled on December 5, there was great uneasiness in the operation's headquarters.

The strike group, which was to take off at 2:30 A.M., would have to fly most of the way in darkness. To succeed at this, good weather was essential. To find out conditions, a weather plane left at 8:30 P.M. December 7. Another left two hours later. On board this second aircraft was a special passenger, Koichi Shimada, a staff officer of the Eleventh Air Fleet. Shimada flew high above the ocean toward the Philippines and judged the weather good. He reported by air: "Departure possible."

This transmission was detected in Manila. The Japanese discovered this when the Takao Naval Communications troops detected a warning alarm being sent from Manila to Clark and Iba fields. In addition, the radio frequency of the plane carrying staff officer Shimada started to be jammed from Manila.

At this detection of their intentions, the leaders of the operation became even more uneasy. And they were shocked when another radio message from the American air base was intercepted by Takao communications. This message was an order to a flight captain of the American air force to take off immediately with three fighters.

This was taken to mean that the Americans were now fully alert to the possibility of the Japanese attack. It also indicated that the American fighters must be extremely good if they had the capability and the skill to fight in the dark.

The operation's leaders became extremely worried now. They had great confidence in the Zero, but their planes would be at a disadvantage having to fight after such a long flight. And the odds looked even worse with the news that the Americans were prepared to intercept at night.

Then came an even more alarming development. The weather changed. After midnight, thick fog closed in on Tainan Base. Takao base was enveloped half an hour later. Takeoff at 2:30 became impossible. The departure had to be postponed until the fog cleared. That meant the loss of surprise.

The first glimmer of dawn came. All of the bases were upset. After the success of Pearl Harbor, they began to hear of the landings on the Malay Peninsula. Further news came that Type 96 land-based torpedo bombers of the Biholo Air Groups of the navy's Twenty-Second Air Flotilla had carried out night bombing on Singapore. The Japanese offensive had already spread to every area.

The operation's leaders could only pray that the fog would let up. The more their attack was prolonged, the better prepared the Americans would be. Resistance would be furious after the strike force's long flight to Luzon from Formosa. There was also the possibility that the B-17s stationed near Manila would strike at Formosa first. The Japanese planes were all sitting on the ground in formation, waiting to take off. If attacked by the B-17s now, the damage would be heavy, and the effect that might have on Japan's overall strategy disastrous.

As if to confirm these fears, at 8 A.M. the Japanese picked up an American message about three B-17s approaching Formosa. It appeared they were on a reconnaissance, but it might also be the beginning of an attack. The head officers at the bases started losing their calm.

Then, at 7 A.M., the fog showed signs of thinning. Spirits began to rise, and in no time, the fog was gone. At once the order to launch was given. Waiting aircrews began to run and jumped into their aircraft. Instantly the sound of starting engines broke the quiet of the airfields, and eighty-four Zeros took off from the Tainan and Takao airfields to escort 108 Type 96 and Type 1 land-based torpedo bombers. At 8:45, the force turned its nose to the Philippine Islands.

A great transoceanic flight by single-seated fighters had just begun. And it was heading toward American bases that were well-prepared to intercept.

Above the ocean spreading without end below them, the combined force of fighters and bombers flew in a great roar of engines. In one way, a great clash of technologies was about to take place, for all the aircraft in the formation were Nagoya Aircraft Works designs. Jiro Horikoshi had designed the Zeros and the Type 96 aircraft, Suero Honjo the Type 1 bombers. And now their designs were about to meet head-on with American aircraft, this time ready for an attack.

The thirty-four Zeros of the Tainan Naval Air Corps, headed by Lieutenant Shingo, flew toward Clark Field. At 1:30 P.M. they reached the Philippines, climbed to 7,000 meters, and deployed for attack. The pilots were expecting to meet a great number of American fighters, because they knew surprise had been lost with the news of Pearl Harbor reaching Manila. However, when the Zeros came over Clark Field, they beheld a miraculous sight.

The Americans had in fact been waiting for a Japanese attack since early morning. But however long they waited, no Japanese, to their surprise, appeared. Finally, the fighters had to land to refuel. They were in the midst of that operation when Shingo's Zeros suddenly appeared. In the end the delay that had made the Japanese wring their hands had turned out to be in Shingo's favor.

A first group of twenty-seven Type 1 torpedo bombers, led by the Zeros, set to bombing the field. They were followed by another group of twenty-seven. The P-40 fighters and B-17 bombers arranged on the airfield, and many buildings and hangars were blasted and burned.

The Zeros circling above the bombers found no fighters, so they descended to strafe the field. At that moment, as if they had been waiting for the chance, five Curtiss P-40 fighters suddenly dived on the Zeros from above.

The Zeros became aware of them. They made a quick turn at high speed and engaged the P-40s, the representative fighter of the U.S. Army, in conditions that initially were against the Zeros. It was the first real fight against American fighters following Pearl Harbor. However, the difference between the two makes of fighter quickly became all too plain. Though speeds were about the same, against the nimbleness of the Zeros the P-40s appeared to fly in confusion. In no time, all five attackers had been downed.

Iba Airfield was attacked by fifty Zeros led by Lieutenant Tamotsu Yokoyama of the Takao Naval Air Corps. They strafed repeatedly the twenty-five American aircraft parked there and destroyed them. Then, on their way to Clark Field, at 4,000 meters they encountered Iba's pursuit squadron of more than ten P-40s and P-35s. Here too, the Zero showed its superlative qualities, shooting down at least ten of the American fighters. Then Yokoyama's planes joined the strafing of Clark Field.

The transoceanic air operation to Luzon Island had ended in a complete victory. In the air battle that day, of the 160 planes of the U.S. Army's air force, sixty had been shot down, burned, or destroyed. Only three Zeros were missing. The Zeros, still keeping watch for fighters, turned back for Formosa with the bombers. They landed after the bombers in the evening sunshine.

The bases were in an uproar. The operation's leaders, who had been so ill at ease, were all now excited at results far beyond their expectations. And they confirmed to each other that the success of the operation was due to the superior performance of the Zero. It was the day the Zero, produced in a country believed by the Americans to be backward in aeronautical technology, gave U.S. aeronautics a shocking blow.

The tremendous superiority of the Zero's range was demonstrated next day, December 9. On that day, thick fog suspended Japanese naval air force sorties from southern Formosa. However, the U.S. forces in the Philippines were reported to be actively preparing for an attack by the Japanese. They were carrying out reconnaissance flights on a large scale over the seas around the Philippines. It appeared there were a considerable number of search planes involved. Monitored messages revealed that they were looking for Japanese aircraft carriers.

By the U.S. standard, it was impossible that the Japanese fighters had come all the way from Formosa, escorting bombers. They believed that the fighters would have had to be launched from carriers near the Philippines. Gradually the search spread to the China Sea, and as it continued persistently for a few days, the naval air force leaders on Formosa smiled.

Meanwhile the superiority of the Zero over American planes was once again demonstrated on December 10. At 10:50 A.M., thirty-four Zeros under Lieutenant Yokoyama took off from Takao Air Base under the guidance of three reconnaissance planes. Again they headed for the Philippines, and since this was their second raid, they were confident of their fuel consumption rate. When they reached the American air force bases they found they could strafe thoroughly and repeatedly with composure. Then, however, they were attacked by scores of P-40s and P-35s. The Zeros were outnumbered by almost two to one.

Like shooting stars, the Zeros kept on zooming up, making quick turns and chasing the American fighters. In vain the American pilots tried to catch the agile Zeros, and in the end, the result was miserable for them. After forty-five minutes, the ferocious dogfight ended with forty-four American fighters shot down, two-thirds of their number. The remaining fighters fled in terror and disappeared.

However, because the combat had lasted for such a time, the Zeros had consumed great quantities of fuel. And they had spread out during the fight, and did not gather at the predetermined rendezvous preparatory to their return to Formosa.

At 3 P.M. Yokoyama was compelled to head for home with the three fighters that happened to be near. Then the weather got worse. Yokoyama lost sight of even his wing men. Alone he flew over the thick cloud. When he reckoned he was near his destination, he came down into it, but the plane was instantly engulfed by heavy rain. Cape Garanpee, the southern tip of Formosa, which was the landmark he had expected, was not to be found. As the day moved toward sunset his visibility was shut down completely by the rain. Yokoyama sensed death. Fuel was running out. Then the engine stopped.

Death was coming close to Lieutenant Tamotsu Yokoyama, who had ferried the 12Si fighter to China for the first time. The wind was screaming, and waves ran high on the gloomy sea. Yokoyama made a forced landing in the rough waters. The shock was heavy. But he was lucky. Just in front of where he landed a Japanese fishing boat drafted to patrol duty was rolling in the waves as it cruised. The fishermen saved him. He had come down off southern Formosa.

Yokoyama was not the only Zero pilot to face disaster. Six planes were lost or had to make forced landings. Among the twenty-eight planes remaining of the thirty-four-plane force, twenty-seven landed at Koushun Base south of Takao Base. One barely reached Batan Islands in the sea south of Formosa. One Zero had been lost in combat.

On that same day, fifty-seven Type 96 torpedo bombers and twenty-six Type 1 torpedo bombers of the Genzan Air Group, the Bihoro Air Group of the Twenty-Second Air Flotilla, and the Kanoya Air Group of the Twenty-First Naval Air Flotilla, based in southern Indochina, launched their attack on the British navy's Eastern Fleet.

England had suspected that the outbreak of war with Japan was close and brought the *Prince of Wales,* one of its newest battleships, and the battle cruiser *Repulse* to the Far East, where they were based at Singapore. On December 8, as soon as war broke out, they left Singapore and headed north to attack the Japanese convoys making landings at Singora on the Malay Peninsula.

At 3:15 P.M. of December 9, the Japanese submarine *I-65* spotted these ships with four destroyers and reported them to the Saigon base. Aircraft and submarines tried to keep contact with them but they lost sight of the British Fleet in rainy weather. The Japanese navy concentrated on finding them.

Next day, December 10, at 3:41 A.M., the submarine *I-58* found the ships again and shadowed them for almost an hour before losing sight of them. The navy's search for the two big capital ships now became frantic. Not until 11:45 A.M. of that same morning, did a navy patrol plane at last locate the British fleet, enabling the land-based attack planes to take off for them.

The result was glorious. First the battle cruiser *Repulse* was sunk, followed by the *Prince of Wales,* one of the newest and most powerful ships of the British navy. Vice Admiral Sir Tom Phillips, commander in chief of the Far Eastern Fleet, was drowned, along with many other seamen. With this battle, the Japanese navy had secured command of the sea the third day after the start of the war. Both the air corps based at Tainan and Takao in southern Formosa again attacked Clark Field, Iba, and other air force bases on the thirteenth of December. DelCarmen and Nichols fields were attacked on the fourteenth. Almost no enemy planes counterattacked. Japan had command of the air over the Philippines.

The advance of the army went smoothly, too. Guam Island, Wake Island, Hong Kong, and Manila were all occupied. Within one month of its commencement the giant Southern Operation was proceeding on schedule. At that time the Zero fighters of the Third Air Group moved to Davao on Mindanao Island as the army secured strategic points. The Tainan Air Corps moved to Jolo Base in the Sulu Archipelago, south of Borneo.

The distance from the Tainan Air Base to the Jolo base was 1,200 nautical miles. It was well beyond the standard range of any single-seat fighter in the world, but in another demonstration of their superb range, all twenty-seven Zeros took off from Tainan and landed at Jolo after six hours.

Meanwhile, the Royal Air Force concentrated around Singapore was suffering miserably. Their airfields were damaged by Japanese bombers. The American Brewster Buffalo, their principal fighter, was no match for the Zero. Then the Hawker Hurricane, which had so distinguished itself in the Battle of Britain, confronted the Zero. But the Hurricane also suffered too easily at the hands of the Zero. The morale of the Royal Air Force rapidly sank. And then it changed into a violent terror of the Zero. Fighter pilots began avoiding combat with the Zero at any cost. To the air forces of America and England, the Zero was beginning to be a mysterious entity.

Fourteen

On December 8, the men of the Nagoya Aircraft Works, already informed of the outbreak of the war through a special newscast, were engulfed with excitement on hearing of the success of the landing operations in Malaya following the surprise attack on Pearl Harbor. Their excitement was the greater knowing that the key weapon of the attacks on the Americans in Hawaii and the Philippines and on the British navy's Far Eastern Fleet was the Zero fighter, and the Type 96 and Type 1 torpedo bombers made by their own hands. They were deeply impressed by the military aircraft of Japan. Until ten years ago Japan had had to invite engineers from foreign countries for guidance in design, or purchase licenses for production. Now they dominated the American aircraft they had been most afraid of.

The production of Type 96 land-based torpedo bombers had already been discontinued, and in its place, the Type 1 and Zero fighters were now in mass production. The Nagoya works had sent out 151 of each aircraft by the end of 1941. But though it was clear these two aircraft had played a major part in the great victories of December 1941, a faint shadow of uneasiness was on the faces of the leaders of the works.

They were well aware of the great scale and high production standards of American industry. Compared with these, Japanese industry was considerably behind and poor in resources. If the war were to be prolonged, it would become a war of industrial strength, and that would obviously go against Japan.

At that time, Jiro Horikoshi, chief designer of the Zero, was absent on account of illness. He had fallen ill, just after he had successfully completed the design and development of the Type 96 carrier-borne fighter. In early September 1941, he was again forced to leave his work. Horikoshi was prone to contracting pleurisy. After a while he had been able to come to the office for short times, but just after the war broke out, he was seized with a sharp pain in his chest that made breathing difficult, and he had to stay in bed for a long time. Overwork without rest in developing the Type 96 and Zero fighters had ruined his health.

A kind of perplexity had sprung into his mind when he heard of the outbreak of war. Horikoshi had toured foreign aircraft companies ten years ago. He had seen inside U.S. aircraft factories with his own eyes. The size of those factories had not struck him as amazingly big at the time, however he had sensed the strength of the American industrial complex supporting them. Once war started, the energy of the people in the factories surely would be concentrated on the production of military weapons using their high degree of mechanization. Military aircraft would begin to pour out of the factories like a rapid stream. America, rich in resources, manufacturing facilities, transportation, and an understanding of mechanization, would easily make that possible.

Horikoshi was ill at ease. Military leaders had mentioned "total war," but considering America's powerful industrial strength, it seemed to him almost impossible for Japan to stand against the United States even if it concentrated all its energies. Of course, Japanese military leaders must have known of the hugeness and sophistication of American industry. They must have calculated that America would oppose Japan with quantity and quality backed by their enormous industrial power.

The Japanese army and navy shared a deep belief in the idea of quality rather than quantity. When it came to aerial fighting, they relied completely on the excellence of their aircrews and aircraft.

Horikoshi thought the navy especially must be planning to use mainly the Zero to confront the quantities of American fighters.

Horikoshi had, of course, been overjoyed at the successes of the Zero. But aeronautical technology progressed rapidly. American aircraft designers would be devoting themselves to their work with a new energy. Horikoshi was upset to remain idle, because once a war broke out, he was sure the American designers would concentrate all their power on designing and developing a fighter to outmatch the Zero. They would be doing so under very favorable circumstances and conditions, and at the end, they would produce them in conveyor belt-style mass production.

It made Horikoshi uneasy to think that his Zero fighter had become the main weapon of naval fighters and that so much was expected of it. As if to shake off this concern, however, the Zero fighter continued to perform wonderfully and to break again and again the bounds of its capabilities on the fields of war.

In February 1942, the main island of Borneo was completely occupied by the Japanese, who planned an attack on Java. The purpose of invading Java was to prevent the island from becoming a fortress for the enemy and also to obtain intact the oil field at Palembang, adjoining Sumatra.

The operation started with attacks by naval fighters on February 3. The air bases around Surabaya in Java were held by the air force of Dutch Indonesia. It consisted of three types of American fighters, the Curtiss P-40 and P-35, and the Brewster Buffalo. A reconnaissance by a Type 98 reconnaissance plane located almost 100 fighters on these fields. At this news, the Zero pilots became excited. Since the big fights over the Philippines they had been engaged only in small-scale combats. They looked forward to a big battle.

The main attack force was to be the Zeros of the Tainan Naval Air Corps, which had advanced its base to Balikpapan in Dutch Borneo. In addition, twenty-seven Zeros based at Manado on the island of Celebes under Lieutenant Yokoyama's leadership were also joined to the operation. The whole force of about sixty fighters was assembled at Balikpapan under Lieutenant Shingo.

Once more, it was going to be a long distance for the Zeros. The distance to Surabaya was 430 nautical miles, and there was unsteady weather to cause anxiety, too. However, it was imperative to destroy the Dutch air force as early as possible and so it was decided to dare the weather and attack anyway.

Fortunately, a reconnaissance plane reported good weather. The Zeros took off from Balikpapan at 8:30 A.M. Following a Type 98 reconnaissance plane, the Zeros flew south in a tight formation, keeping to an altitude of 4,000 meters. After about three hours the green-covered island of Java came in sight. Gradually the Zeros lost altitude. At 11:30 A.M. the formation deployed for attack and rushed all together into the skies above Surabaya. Their enemies were waiting for them, glinting in the sky like a cloud of tinfoil. The Zeros increased their speed and dashed into these bright spots. A large and fierce combat broke out in the skies over the city of Surabaya.

This combat was quite different from the confrontation over Chungking. The Chinese fighters had been surprised by the Zeros when they made a sudden return after the bombing raid. The fighters of the Dutch Indonesian air force were ready for them almost at the same altitude in an interception formation. For once, no surprise was involved as the Zeros faced the challenge of superior numbers after a long sea flight. This was to be a real test of the Zero against American aeronautical technology.

More than 160 fighters were fighting in the sky, diving, looping, zooming among each other. Pieces of duralumin of those planes that were disintegrating burst out like flowers in the sky. Tracer fire from machine guns crisscrossed, flames burst, black smoke trails came from planes going down.

As time elapsed, it seemed the Zeros in the sky were rapidly increasing in number. But that was an illusion caused by the rapidly decreasing numbers of American fighters. And in no time, only the graceful forms of the Zeros were left circling over Surabaya.

The Zeros assembled in small groups and turned their noses to the north. Fading wisps and trails of black smoke were the only signs remaining of the air combat.

The results of that fight were thirty-five confirmed downings of American fighters, fifteen unconfirmed, and four flying boats burned at their moorings by strafing. One B-17 had also been destroyed on the ground. The Zeros had lost three. The Dutch Indonesian air force had been destroyed. Japan had completely secured air superiority over all Indonesia.

At the same time, other operations against the Dutch, British, and U.S. forces defending Indonesia produced complete victories. In the battle of the Java sea, a combined Australian, British, Dutch, and American fleet was largely destroyed without loss to the Japanese navy. And in other sea battles off Surabaya and Batavia, the surviving warships were destroyed. A drop of parachutists on the Palembang oilfield secured that intact, and the Japanese army occupied Java almost without resistance. Thirteen thousand Dutch, British, and Australian soldiers surrendered. The Dutch surrendered in Indonesia on March 9.

The first four months of war had brought successes beyond the expectations of Japan's military leaders. The surprise attack on Pearl Harbor had dealt a serious blow to the U.S. Navy. Most of the strategic points of the three colonial powers in the Far East had fallen into Japanese hands. And Japan had secured complete air superiority in this vast area.

Since Hawaii, the Zero had been the main battle plane of the Naval Air Corps. In the first four months of the war, up to the surrender of the Dutch in Indonesia, the Naval Air Corps had downed 565 Dutch, British, and American planes. Of this total, Zeros had claimed 471—83 percent of the total. The major victories in Hawaii, the Philippines, and in the East Indies had been the consequence of the Zero's excellence and the tactical planning. And at the end of this campaign, the Zero had acquired a fearful reputation among the British, Dutch, and Americans.

They had known of a Japanese fighter with a range great enough to fly from Hankow to Chungking. They had heard of the great numbers of Russian-made I-15s and I-16s, shot down as if the aircraft were merely playing at dogfighting. They had known also that the Zeros had suffered almost no losses in these one-sided combats. Still, they did not believe a country as backward as Japan, reliant on imported technology, could, in a few short years, produce an advanced aircraft on its own. Japan was an inferior country. Its pilots were not even as skillful as the Chinese pilots. So when the Zero suddenly appeared in front of European and American pilots, they faced it with arrogant confidence.

They were sure they could demolish the fighter. But when a fight began, they noticed how quickly a Zero came at them. And after a moment of maneuvering they saw the amazing climbing and turning ability that brought the Zero up behind them. Then they got a taste of the tremendous firepower that no one had imagined such a light and slender plane could possess.

It was unbelievable. The pilots could not imagine that their own fighters, produced by the most industrially advanced countries, should be almost useless against the fighter from Japan, a little island country. Even worse, they could not believe that their own skills as pilots were inferior to those of the Japanese. They had their pride. It could not be that they would lose the fight. They were confused, but they went on challenging the Zero.

Then the time came when their confidence collapsed. Each time they fought, they were damaged beyond recovery. Then they developed a terrible fear of the Zero. To them, the Zero was not a plane but a strange and mysterious flying object. One pilot even said that each time he fought against the Zero, it seemed the aircraft of his side were racing one another to go down by themselves. Pilots gave up fighting the Zero and even actively fled from it.

The successes of the first four months of the war showed that there was no one kind of fighter among the Zero's opponents that could match it. And it was not the only great Japanese plane. In Malaya, the Type 1 fighter (code name: Oscar), built for the army by the Nakajima Aircraft Company, was also scoring glorious results. Both army and navy aircraft were proving themselves above the world standard.

Fifteen

The Nagoya Aircraft Works of Mitsubishi Heavy Industries were devoted to the production of military airplanes. The facilities were at maximum utilization. The working area of the works was enlarged to 150,000 *tsubo* (1 *tsubo* = 3.3 square meters) in May of 1942, an area seven times the size of the works at the time of the Japan-China incident in July 1937. The number of workers increased five-fold, to 30,000.

The engine division had already been separated in July 1938, and operated independently of the Nagoya works in facilities at the northern end of Nagoya. Then, in 1941, the army and navy ordered a second expansion, the construction of the Kumamoto and Mizushima Aircraft Works. These were government projects to be run by Mitsubishi.

At the Kumamoto works, the construction of factories totalling 130,000 *tsubo* was planned on a 440,000-*tsubo* site. A further 570,000-*tsubo* site was secured by the army for an airfield. The Mizushima Works were even larger in scale, 1,400,000 *tsubo*. This included the factory site and an airfield, made at the request of the navy by reclaiming land from the sea about nine kilometers south of Kurashiki, in Okayama Prefecture. There were also plans to enlarge the Nagoya Aircraft Works yet more by purchasing the Nagoya factory of the

Nisshin Spinning Company. The construction of extra plants for military aircraft manufacture did not stop there. The army was constructing the 400,000-*tsubo* Chita hangar and airfield on the Chita Peninsula in Aichi Prefecture for testing and maintaining its own planes.

The works were alive with a sense of purpose, fueled by the spectacular successes of the war. Especially attracting the workers' attention was news of the air war. People became excited seeing pictures of the planes they had manufactured, or in which they had installed engines. Many shed tears at news of overwhelming victories.

The works contained factories for both army and navy planes. The employees of each branch raced each other in production. The rivalry was open. The army planes under construction at the Nagoya works were the Type 97 heavy bomber (code name: Sally), the Type 100 reconnaissance plane (code name: Dinah), and the Type 99 scout plane (code name: Sonia). Navy planes being built were the Zero and the Zero sea scout plane.

Among the fighters, more Zeros were produced than any other. In 1942, the works smoothly put out sixty in January, fifty-eight in February, fifty-five in March. And at the Nakajima Aircraft Company, also making Zeros, the number of planes produced rose steadily: nineteen in January, twenty-two in February, and thirty-five in March. The number of Type 1 torpedo bombers also increased, twenty-five in January, twenty-seven in February, and thirty in March.

The work force in the factories had a high morale. The day started at 6:30 A.M., when everyone flowed into the gates of the Nagoya works. Work started at 7 A.M. Closing time was 4:30, but most people stayed on longer. Overtime had become routine.

The number of oxcarts used to transport the airframes was increasing rapidly. Just after sunset, oxcarts loaded with fuselages or wings came out in a string from the gate of the works. Heavers with lamps in their hands surrounded the carts. The chain of lanterns moved slowly in the night through Nagoya. When they came to the Nunobike area, the U.S. Consulate, of course, was no longer a worry. With the outbreak of the war, the staff of the consulate had been detained by the Japanese government, so there was nobody to stealthily watch the oxcarts. The guard on the carts was still tight, however. Fuselages and wings were tightly shrouded in canvas. Policemen stood at key points and looked over the passing carts.

In spite of all the construction and expansion in aircraft manufacture in Nagoya, no improvement to the road on which the oxcarts travelled was planned. The bad roads were accepted as a matter of course. And they got worse as rising production used more and more carts. After a rainfall, they were especially muddy, and the carts often got stuck. It still took twenty-four hours to go the forty-eight kilometers from the works to the Kagamigahara Airfield.

The oxen were working hard, too. As the number of journeys increased, the oxen grew more and more tired. To help them when an airframe had been delivered, the oxen were trucked back to Nagoya, to save them the long walk back. They were well fed so they would recover quickly from fatigue. Seiichiro Tamura, the transportation supervisor, ordered beer and made the oxen drink it in the trucks on the drive back.

The Nagoya works were visited successively by Admiral Shigetaro Shimada, the Minister of the navy; General Hajime Sugiyama, chief of the general staff of the army at the Imperial General Headquarters; and Prince Takamatsu, commander of the Yokosuka Naval Air Corps. Factory workers gained the impression that they had an important position in the war from the visits of such distinguished persons.

Jiro Horikoshi had at last recovered from his illness and began to go back to work. He was occupied with the design of the navy's 14Si interceptor fighter (later named the Raiden, code name: Jack). Horikoshi led the design team—almost the same team that had worked on the Zero.

The Raiden was an interceptor fighter, and therefore was required to have only a small range. Its maximum speed, however, was to be 600 kilometers per hour at 6,000 meters. It also had to be able to climb to 6,000 meters in five minutes, thirty seconds, carry an armament of two sets of 7.7-millimeter machine guns and twenty-millimeter cannons, and for a power plant, the Kasei Type 13 engine made by Mitsubishi had to be installed. This engine was reliable, though its diameter was too large for a fighter.

Work on the Raiden, however, had been seriously interrupted by the investigation of the midair disintegration of Zero number 135 (April 1941) and the designing of improvements. Then engineer Yoshitoshi Sone, Horikoshi's most reliable subordinate, had come down with a chest disease, and following that, Horikoshi himself had become ill. In mid-September, engineer Mijiro Takahashi took over from Horikoshi as the Raiden's chief designer, by which time the basic design had been finished.

Under Takahashi's leadership, the design group for the 14Si fighter showed unusual enthusiasm. The number one prototype flew for the first time on March 20, 1942, and entered the stage of flight testing. Horikoshi was present at the flight test, but Takahashi remained as chief designer of the 14Si fighter.

A month later, on April 14, Horikoshi attended a conference held at the Naval Aeronautical Engineering Establishment. He was still pale and recovering from his illness. The meeting was the first to study the 17Si carrier-borne fighter (later called the Reppu, code name: Sam).

This single-seat carrier-borne fighter was intended to be faster and more powerfully armed than the Zero. Horikoshi, who had expended all his energy on developing and improving the Zero, was given the heavy burden of designing and developing the plane to the navy's requirements, once more severe.

The Zero was the best all-purpose fighter in the world, but its engine was of small power because agility came first. Speed and climbing ability had been sacrificed to some extent. Such a design inevitably had no room to spare for armor or strengthened armaments. To improve on this, there were two choices: increase the power of the engine to the limit bearable by the airframe, or develop a new fighter able to carry a larger engine. Otherwise, superiority over the American fighters would not last long. In other words, the 17Si fighter, or Reppu, was meant to succeed the Zero.

In spite of the Zero's great superiority, now bordering on the mysterious to Japan's foes, progress in aeronautical technology around the world was still dazzlingly rapid. The U.S. Air Force in particular, having been made to look foolish by the Zero, could be counted on to make an all-out effort to develop a fighter that would match it. The designers of American fighters by now would have clearly realized that they had been absolutely beaten in competition with Japanese designers on the field of war. They had had great confidence in themselves, but now they had learned that their confidence was only an illusion.

The Americans would be pouring a huge effort into new designs, and they would be backed up by America's immense industrial strength.

The Japanese aeronautical staffs expected that sooner or later, fighters equal to the Zero would appear. They had information that a

U.S. Army fighter called the Lockheed P-38 was already in mass production. The P-38 seemed to them a little strange. It was twin-engined and twin-boomed, with an unusually high performance at high altitude. Its two liquid-cooled engines of 1,150 horsepower each had exhaust-driven turbosuperchargers, the first in the world.

The Japanese navy's aeronautical staff hoped for a fighter with the Zero's range, but even greater superiority in its performance. The 17Si fighter was to provide this requirement. At the meeting to discuss it, the navy testified again that the Zero was the best in the world. Then it emphasized that the 17Si fighter had also to be able to absolutely dominate any American fighter that should turn up, as the Zero had done.

Horikoshi insisted on the adoption of the MK9A engine of larger power, now under development by Mitsubishi. The adoption would depend on his experiences, progress in technology, and the changing war situation. But the Naval Aeronautical Headquarters said it was their wish to use the NK9H engine by Nakajima (later developed as the Homare engine). In the end, these differences were left to future study.

At that time, Horikoshi was asked by Lieutenant Commander Osamu Nagano, in charge of aero engines on the technical staff of the Naval Aeronautical Headquarters, if he was willing to exchange the Zero's Sakae 12 engine for the larger Kinsei engine by Mitsubishi. Besides the Zero, the Sakae 12 was also being installed in the army's Type 99 light bomber (code name: Lily) and the Type 1 fighter, and was now at the limit of its production in meeting these demands. It might happen that needs could not be satisfied if production were required to grow still further. Nakano was suggesting that it was better to avoid the risk beforehand.

Horikoshi saw no reason to object, rather, he agreed strongly with Nagano. However, Horikoshi was not in a position to approve of this change.

The navy had assigned certain projects to the Nagoya works—the improvement of the Type 1 land-based torpedo bomber, design and research for its successor, improvement of the Zero sea scout plane, and development of a 17Si interceptor fighter. All this was beside Horikoshi's own responsibility for the 17Si carrier-borne fighter, the Reppu.

Within the Nagoya Aircraft Works, responsible for so many projects, Horikoshi's own design group had a heavy load. They had to make improvements to the Zero in accordance with the requests of the battlefield flying corps, complete the 14Si interceptor just developed (the Raiden), and newly design the 17Si carrier-borne fighter (the Reppu). And each of these projects had been assigned a first priority status.

This was a problem. The navy made no distinction between aircraft projects that were urgent, and ones not urgent. All were called urgent. Every airplane design group had to work with this clash of priorities. As a result, designers were fully taken up with their assigned tasks, and had no time to spare for new projects. Had the navy cared about this situation, Mitsubishi could have assigned its design engineers and others proper project priorities and the projects would have proceeded smoothly. But without clear guidance from the navy, it was difficult for the company to do so. Of course Horikoshi wanted to begin designing the installation of the Kinsei engine for the Zero and start on the 17Si carrier-borne fighter, too. But amid the clash of priorities, it was impossible to do so.

There were such troubles at home, but meanwhile, the operations of the naval corps overseas were extremely active. After the capture of Wake Island (December 23, 1941) the Japanese Naval Air Corps had scored a great victory with the occupation of Rabaul. Wide-ranging attacks on Port Darwin, Australia, and on Ceylon had followed. These proved how complete was the air superiority over most of the southern Pacific secured by the Japanese navy and army. But now the first stage of the war was finished, and a lull followed.

In Japan, measures were taken to put the country more strongly on a war footing, with good control ordinances and a ticket rationing system for clothing. Companies were rearranged. Many minor enterprises were dissolved, and their workers drafted to munitions factories. The military began to intervene openly in the mass media. One by one, these measures concentrated the energies of the Japanese people on the war.

Then, just after 1 P.M. on April 18, 1942, an unimaginable incident happened that doused the victorious mood of the Japanese people with cold water. On that day, strange twin-engined aircraft came flying slowly and at a low altitude over Tokyo. The citizens looked up curiously at the star marking on the wings of the planes. There was no alarm. The people had no idea that these were American bombers.

The twin-engined craft were American army B-25 Mitchell bombers, under the command of Lieutenant Colonel James A. Doolittle. They had been launched from the aircraft carrier *Hornet,* which had approached to a point 668 miles east of Cape Inubo in company with another carrier, the *Enterprise*. The bombers had skimmed the sea to approach Tokyo.

There were thirteen bombers. Another three headed for Nagoya and western Japan. At Nagoya, too, the citizens did not recognize the aircraft overhead as American. In the town, people came and went as usual. Tramcars and buses were operating; at the sports ground, citizens could be seen playing games.

One of the B-25s approached the Nagoya Aircraft Works at low altitude and suddenly dropped something metallic. There was a great explosion. Flame and smoke leapt into the air. Workers at the factories were surprised at the sound, but they thought it was an accidental explosion. Most kept on working. The bomber had dropped incendiary bombs. Damage to the factory was light, but five workers were instantly killed, nine severely injured, and another twenty-one slightly injured.

Of the sixteen B-25s in this first bold raid on Japan's mainland, three ran out of fuel in an area of China occupied by Japan. Eight crewmen bailed out. A fourth plane made an emergency landing in Soviet territory. The remaining twelve planes reached the Lishui Airfield in China, but failed to make good night landings. All were severely damaged.

Though the raid was a complete surprise to the citizens of Tokyo and Nagoya, the Japanese navy had had a suspicion it might occur. At 6:30 A.M. on April 10, eight days before the raid took place, the navy's Owada communication station had monitored a coded order transmitted by what appeared to be two or three American aircraft carriers stealthily approaching the Japanese mainland. From this the suspicion arose that the task force was going to launch an air raid on Tokyo.

The combined fleet ordered patrol planes at Kisarazu and Minami Torishima to search for the enemy within a range of 700 nautical miles and quickly began to plan a counter attack. The plan was to find the American force the day before the planned air raid and attack them with torpedos. Meanwhile, Vice Admiral Nagumo's task force, then returning home from operations in the Indian Ocean, was to be sent to attack the American fleet.

The plan depended on the patrol planes locating the Americans, but the patrol network turned up nothing until 6:30 A.M., April 18. Then an urgent report came in from number 23 patrol boat, *Nitto Maru:* "Enemy aircraft carriers in sight." Unfortunately, the Americans detected this signal, and the *Nitto Maru* was immediately attacked by a cruiser and carrier planes and sunk before the Japanese could prepare to intercept.

Judging from the position of the American carriers, the navy decided that the air raid would take place on April 19. The American task force, however, alarmed by the *Nitto Maru's* discovery of it, decided at once to shift the launch date ahead to the eighteenth, and within two hours of *Nitto Maru's* 6:30 A.M. sighting *Hornet* had launched the B-25s, and the task force was changing course to escape. This decision baffled the intentions of the Japanese navy and made it easy for the bombers to reach Japan.

Though the damage from the Doolittle raid was small, the loss of face for the Japanese navy was great, for it had repeatedly stated that it could be relied on to defend the Japanese homeland. This was most embarrassing for the navy's leaders. And then embarrassment turned into two operations.

One aimed at not allowing the Americans to repeat their surprise raid. The raid had only been possible because carrier-launched bombers had been able to fly on from Japan to a friendly air base at Lishui on the Chinese mainland. Imperial Headquarters now ordered the capture of this airfield and others. Immediately ground troops launched an attack in cooperation with the air force and in spite of heavy counterattacks by the Chinese the airfields were captured.

The second operation was a grand campaign carried out at the insistence of the commander in chief of the combined fleet, Admiral Isoroku Yamamoto. Yamamoto had been deeply shocked by the Doolittle raid. To prevent further raids, he decided it would be necessary to capture bases on remote Midway Island and the equally remote Aleutian Islands in the North Pacific. The Americans had an air base on Midway, and also one at Dutch Harbor in the Aleutians. These were the most forward bases the Americans had from which they could launch planes against Japan. Possession of them by the Japanese would prevent raids from being launched.

Yamamoto had larger objectives in this scheme, too. The American Pacific Fleet was still weak after its huge losses at Pearl Harbor. Yamamoto hoped to draw out the remainder of the fleet in defense of these bases and annihilate it, as he felt certain he could do, since he proposed to commit almost the entire force of fighting ships in the Japanese navy—more than 160 warships and auxiliaries, not including small craft. If Japan were victorious in the campaign, it would be able to raid Pearl Harbor from Midway, and above all, gain the time needed to occupy many more key places in the Pacific and make its defenses very strong before the United States replaced losses and counterattacked.

Yamamoto's plan was vigorously opposed by other navy leaders, but his will was strong, and in the end Imperial General Headquarters agreed with him. On May 5, 1942, it gave the order to capture Midway Island and strategic positions in the southern Aleutian Islands in cooperation with the army.

The theater of operations was divided in two. One was the Midway theater, the other the Aleutian theater. Yamamoto's huge fleet was broken up into five powerful groups. The advance group consisted of sixteen submarines. The main body was composed of seven battleships—*Nagato, Mutsu, Ise, Hyuga, Yamashiro, Fuso,* and the 70,000 ton *Yamato*—the biggest battleship in the world, and also the most powerful with its gigantic eighteen-inch guns. *Yamato* was also Yamamoto's flagship. Accompanying these battleships were the light carrier *Hosho,* three light cruisers, two submarine tenders, and twenty destroyers. With some changes, Vice Admiral Chuichi Nagumo's Hawaii Strike Force formed a third group, with the four aircraft carriers *Akagi, Kaga, Hiryu,* and *Soryu,* escorted by the battleships *Haruna* and *Kirishima,* the heavy cruisers *Tome* and *Chikuma,* and one light cruiser and sixteen destroyers. The attack group, which would capture Midway, was led by Rear Admiral Nobutake Kondo. He commanded two battleships, *Hiei* and *Kongo,* and a force of eight heavy cruisers—*Atago, Chokai, Myoko, Haguro, Kumano, Suzuya, Mikuma,* and *Mogami.* The group also included the aircraft carrier *Zuiho,* two light cruisers and twenty-one destroyers. The attack group shepherded a fleet of sixteen transports carrying the occupation troops. These were 2,800 special marines of the Second Joint Corps and 3,000 soldiers of the Itsuki detached troop. The fifth battle group was the force sent to seize a base on the Aleutians.

Of the surface ship forces, Nagumo's task force was first to depart the Inland Sea at 6 A.M., on May 27, 1942, Naval Memorial Day. The other groups followed successively to the area of Midway Island.

By the time the great fleet had set out, the Americans had been able to decode enough intelligence to piece together an accurate picture of Yamamoto's intentions. They deployed their own fleet accordingly in the Midway area. The much smaller American forces were in two groups. Rear Admiral Raymond Spruance commanded the aircraft carriers *Hornet* and *Enterprise,* five heavy cruisers, and one light cruiser. The carrier *Yorktown,* two heavy cruisers, and five destroyers were under the command of Rear Admiral Frank Fletcher.

The U.S. Navy had been heavily damaged in many sea battles, including the battle of the Coral Sea, which had taken place one month before, in early May. With their fleet so reduced, the Americans did not consider it possible to defeat decisively a Japanese fleet as gigantic as the one on its way to trap them and capture Midway. Attrition, however, was possible, especially of the Japanese aircraft carriers, the key ships in their battle fleet.

The Battle of Midway began at 1:30 A.M. on June 4, when the first Japanese strike wave of 108 aircraft, including thirty-six Zeros, was launched toward Midway. It was led by Lieutenant Takeichi Tomonoga, air group commander of *Hiryu.*

Shortly after the strike wave had been launched from the carriers, they were shadowed by a PBY-5 flying boat. When the force had gotten within thirty miles of Midway, the flying boat suddenly climbed above the strike wave and dropped a parachute with a brilliant flare. It was to guide some fifty-odd American naval fighters, consisting of the Brewster Buffalo and the F4F Wildcat.

Instantly the fighters closed with the strike wave.

The thirty-four escorting Zeros charged into the numerically superior American fighters, and a violent air battle took place. The F4F Wildcat was thought to be the most maneuverable fighter by American pilots. But the Zero fighters completely prevented the American planes from getting close to the bombers, and shot down forty of the attackers. Only two Zeros were lost.

Tomonoga's strike wave raided Midway Island, but encountered no planes on the ground or in the air. Tomonoga judged that it would be necessary to attack again in order to destroy the returned American aircraft that had been evacuated for the raid. He radioed Vice

Admiral Nagumo, commander of his task force group: "A second attack is necessary."

On the decks of Nagumo's four aircraft carriers *Akagi, Kaga, Hiryu,* and *Soryu,* ninety-three planes loaded with torpedos had been kept back for a possible attack on the enemy carriers. Nagumo, however, did not expect to find them in his vicinity until June 7, several days hence—he hoped a diversionary attack on Dutch Harbor on June 3 in the Aleutians would have drawn the carriers north while he occupied Midway. So when Lieutenant Tomonoga's request for a second bombing raid arrived, the decision was made to rearm the torpedo bombers with 800-kilogram bombs for an attack on the island. Ground crews were hard at work on this change and had almost finished the changeover when the heavy cruiser *Tone* radioed: "Ten ships—likely enemy—in sight."

At this news, great confusion broke out on the carriers. Bombs just loaded were unloaded and torpedos loaded again. The change had only just been finished, and the planes had started their engines and were about to launch when suddenly twelve American dive bombers appeared above *Akagi, Kaga,* and *Soryu*. They dropped their bombs.

Only small numbers of bombs hit each ship, but the great number of bombs left on the deck from the changeover exploded. The three ships were instantly engulfed in flame. Then bombs struck *Hiryu,* too, and it exploded.

The four ships stayed afloat for nearly nine hours, but *Kaga* and *Soryu* sank. *Akagi,* still afloat and burning, had to be sunk by the destroyer *Nowaki*. The destroyer *Makigumo* finished off the stricken *Hiryu*.

Before it was struck, *Hiryu* managed to launch its own strike wave of ten attack planes, and six Zeros led by Lieutenant Tomonoga against the carrier *Yorktown*. The carrier was severely damaged by two torpedos and was sunk by the submarine *I-168* later.

At the battle of Midway, Japan's navy suffered a severe defeat. Four of its aircraft carriers, the most important ships in the navy, were lost, along with many skilled pilots and numbers of planes. In addition, the heavy cruiser *Mikuma* was lost. It was the first Japanese defeat since the start of the war.

In fear of the public's shock at this news, military headquarters kept the defeat secret. Even much of the navy was kept in the dark, and only a special few informed. So as to prevent rescued crewmen of the carriers from talking, they were all detained in one place for a time and later given assignments that split them up. In spite of these precautions, however, news of the disaster became widespread, and a dark mood settled over Japan.

At Midway, the navy had been badly beaten, but the Zero was not. It had again proven superior to the American fighters. But then, in the operation to occupy strategic points of the Aleutians, an incident occurred that allowed the Americans at last to study the general configuration of the mysterious Zero fighter.

The Aleutian operation went ahead at the same time as that at Midway. It was partly a diversion. It was hoped that an attack on the base at Dutch Harbor would divert the American carriers north while Nagumo's task force captured Midway. This was therefore the first Japanese force to strike at the Americans in Yamamoto's great plan to annihilate the Pacific Fleet.

Two strike forces were assigned to the Aleutian theater, the Fifth Fleet under Vice Admiral Boshiro Hosogaya and a second force under Rear Admiral Kakuji Kakuda. There were also ground troops for the occupation of Kiska, Attu, and Adak islands. The operation started when Kakuda's force, consisting of the light carriers *Ryujo* and *Junyo,* the heavy cruisers *Takao* and *Maya,* and three destroyers of the Seventh Destroyer Group, left Japan on May 27.

Both forces labored toward the Aleutians in thick fog and heavy weather. On June 3 the second task force had come within 200 miles south of Unalaska Island. On that day and the next, the carriers launched bombers and fighters against the base at Dutch Harbor in the eastern Aleutians. On the seventh, 600 soldiers of the Third Special Marine Corps from Maizuru Naval Station landed on undefended Kiska Island. Attu was also occupied. The operation seemed to have been a success. But the Japanese did not know that during the first air raid on Dutch Harbor on June 3 an unlucky accident for the naval air force had happened.

For the first air raid, both *Junyo* and *Ryujo* had launched strike forces of Zeros and bombers. The strike force from *Junyo,* however, under the command of Lieutenant Toshio Shiga, had had to turn back, intercepted by American fighters and blocked by very bad weather, for which the Aleutians were notorious. Meanwhile, *Ryujo's* force led by Lieutenant Masayuki Yamagami found Dutch Harbor through a break in the cloud. The bombers started attacking radio stations, fuel depots and harbor facilities. Dutch Harbor was instantly covered in black smoke and fires. No enemy fighters were met, so the Zeros strafed flying boats at their moorings.

The accident happened just after that.

The Zero flown by Koga, a flying petty officer first class, was hit in the gasoline tank. The leak was heavy, and it became impossible to return to the carrier. Koga reported to his commander that he would have to make an emergency landing. Suddenly he decreased altitude. Watched by companions, he descended to a small deserted island, east of Dutch Harbor. The island was a predetermined emergency landing spot. A submarine would be dispatched to it with rescue crews.

Watching from above, the commander judged that Koga would land safely. He was maneuvering calmly, and he looked to have chosen a good spot, a flat, grassy stretch of ground. But to his surprise, Koga's plane did a headstand the instant it touched and fell onto its back. It was then the commander realized that what had looked like grass was in fact treacherous muskeg. Koga did not come out of the plane. The commander thought he must be badly wounded, or dead.

Thick fog flowed over the landing position, swallowing the plane. The commander returned to his carrier, *Ryujo,* and reported the crash. A waiting submarine was requested to go to the rescue. The submarine got to the island. Crews landed and searched eagerly. But the weather turned worse and worse, and they had to give up without finding anything.

Later, an American navy search group happened to land on the island and found a Japanese fighter upside down in a muskeg area. It was in almost perfect condition, except for slight damage to the nose and wing tips. They found the pilot still under the canopy, his skull crushed in by the impact.

Their report quickly brought naval researchers to the island. They found that the fighter lying upside down was none other than a Zero—the destroyer of so many American aircraft. They were extremely pleased. The Americans had been collecting fragments of Zeros shot down at Pearl Harbor or in the Philippines in an effort to piece together a specimen of the outstanding, phantom-like fighter. That had not got them far, however. Now, after all their frustration, they suddenly had what they wanted.

Koga's plane was carefully packed and in August 1942 it arrived by sea transport at the assembly and repair department at the Naval Air Station at North Island, San Diego. There it was carefully taken to pieces and studied. The damaged portions were repaired, and the plane reassembled. When it had been perfectly restored, the airframe was painted and the star of the American forces put on the wings and fuselage in place of the Rising Sun. Thus the structural secrets of the Zero were revealed.

Repeated flight tests to research the fighter's performance were made. Comparison tests with the F4F and the F4U-1 fighters of the U.S. Navy were also flown. Then the plane was moved to the army air force's Wright Field. Here too it was matched against army fighters for comparison and performance tests. Finally, the results were distributed to engineers and the pilots of the aircraft companies. The total configuration of the Type Zero fighter Model 21 was now known, and in a final strength test at Wright Field, Koga's captured aircraft was reduced to scrap.

The Americans were surprised at what they found out about the aeronautics of the Zero. They were astonished at the aircraft's 1,000-mile (1,800-mile maximum) range, in spite of its heavy armament of two sets each of 7.7-millimeter machine guns and twenty-millimeter cannons. It was also extremely light at 2,360 kilograms. By comparing its performance with army and navy fighters, the researchers saw clearly the fighter's maneuverability, its refined control touch, and the effect of the rudder in maneuvering in a vertical plane. A U.S. fighter could hardly match the Zero. Above all, they were awakened at last to the level of Japanese aeronautical technology.

However, research had also revealed the defects of a plane that at first had seemed invincible in the flight tests. It had a low limited speed in a deep dive, no protection whatever from bullets, not enough safety devices, insufficient high altitude performance, difficulty at the roll at high speed, and other limitations. Study of these defects made it possible to devise tactics that took advantage of them. The air force also determined to hasten the design of fighters superior to the Zero.

Lieutenant Commander John S. Sati was at the center of devising tactics to counter the Zero. He was the navy's authority on fighter tactics, and had flown the Zero in its first test flight at the North Island Air Base. He had also taken charge of flight tests after that.

He judged that it was impossible to win against the Zero one on one. Two cooperating fighters attacking a Zero could succeed, however. They would take a position higher than the Zero and then both make a deep dive to get in the first blow. If their attack failed, they were never to get involved in a dogfight, since once that began, it was almost impossible to win, even with two against one.

For this reason, after the first blow, the two attacking fighters were to cross each other in escaping. In case the Zero tailed one, the other would attack the Zero from the rear to help the partner escape. Whenever possible, however, the initial deep dive was to be stopped, and the fighters were to keep to an altitude that would not allow the Zero to pursue them and use its superior qualities fighting on the vertical plane. The attackers should wait for another chance from a distance. In other words, the fighters were to work as a team, make a hit and run, and avoid dogfighting.

Though these tactics were meant to take advantage of the Zero's vulnerable points, it could be said that they also demonstrated the surprise of the American aeronautical staffs at the Zero's performance. The Sati tactics were adopted by F4F Wildcat pilots, who were suffering severely in air fighting in the Solomons. Other kinds of fighters also began to adopt them.

The defeat of the Japanese navy at Midway had heavily damaged its power. It had also destroyed at a stroke support in the navy for the big gunship as the decisive force in naval war. From ancient times in the navy, the idea that a war could be decided by battle between fleets had been almost an article of faith. The Japanese, of course, had not been alone among navies in this belief. But it had certainly gone farthest in giving it expression with the construction of the world's largest and most powerful battleships, the *Yamato* and its sister ship *Musashi*.

The fully loaded displacement of each of these super-dreadnoughts was 71,100 tons. Each carried nine eighteen-inch guns—the first time in history that guns of such huge size had been put aboard ships. At the time of Midway, the navy was starting construction of sister ships numbers three and four, and even had plans for monster battleships carrying twenty-inch guns.

The usual enthusiasm in the navy for battleships was quickened by a reliance on gunnery techniques of a very high level. But on the other hand, the adoption of air power as the decisive force at sea, based on Japan's rapid progress in aeronautical technology, had been championed by Admiral Isoroku Yamamoto and Rear Admiral Takijiro Onishi. The superiority of this principle had been clearly demonstrated early in the war with the air raid on Pearl Harbor and the swift destruction of the *Prince of Wales* and *Repulse* and many other vessels attacked by naval aircraft.

As a result of these victories, the number three sister ship of the *Yamato* and *Musashi* under construction at Yokosuka Naval Yard was ordered to be rebuilt as an aircraft carrier instead. The keel of number four sister ship, laid down in the dry dock of Kure Naval Yard, was secretly broken up.

The loss of four regular aircraft carriers had enormously lowered the fighting power of the Japanese navy. On June 30, 1942, less than a month after the Midway disaster, the Naval General Staff announced a program to strengthen the carrier forces. The program approved by the navy minister was extensive. It included advancing the remodeling schedule for the carriers *Hiyo, Ryujo,* and *Chuo* (a former merchant ship) which had originally been due at the end of 1942. The program also called for the number three sister ship of the *Yamato* class super-dreadnoughts under construction at Yokosuka Naval Yard to be converted into a carrier. This vessel, to be called the *Shinano,* was to be ready by October 1, 1944. More conversions would also be made of merchant ships, and there was other new building as well. Air crew training was also stepped up.

Midway had shown how extremely weak an aircraft carrier was against enemy attack. As a result, a reorganization of task fleets was announced on July 14. Carriers would now be combined with battleships and other vessels into one fleet. Also the air corps at Rabaul and other bases were to prepare for interception. These new plans were carried out at once. The Japanese navy devoted itself to consolidating its fighting power.

Only seven months into the war, however, shocking differences were already apparent between the Japanese and U.S. air forces in the means available to them. The number of front-line craft assigned to the newly re-formed Naval Air Corps after the battle of Midway remained at 1,498. This included 492 Zero fighters, in spite of desperate efforts to increase production, which had only produced 184 new

Zeros since the outbreak of the war. Against this, the Americans had planned a great increase in production at the outbreak of the war, and predicted that it was possible to achieve 60 percent of this production target of 60,000 aircraft (including 47,000 fighters) in 1942. They then planned to achieve 70 percent of 125,000 (including 100,000 fighters) in 1943. Of this production, half was to be supplied to England and other allied countries. But even so, the U.S. Air Force had the advantage of being able to concentrate its aircraft in small areas of operation in the Pacific, whereas Japan had to distribute aircraft along the enormous front line of the Soviet-Manchurian border, and in China and the whole recently conquered area to the south—the Philippines, Malaya, Indonesia, and the southern Pacific. This situation made the difference in the strengths and means of the opposing air forces more than a matter of figures. But the fact remained that the difference in U.S. and Japanese industrial strength had already emerged in terms of aircraft.

This was not the only difference. Completely preoccupied with improving and producing current models, the small number of Japanese aircraft designers did not have the resources to develop new aircraft. In the United States, there were many more designers available for this. Working conditions in the factories were good, with good machines and mass production, conveyor-belt systems that made production go smoothly. The Americans could also draw on a population twice the size of Japan's for new pilots.

After Midway, there came a lull in the fighting, and the war between Japan and the United States focused on New Guinea and the Solomon Islands. The Japanese expected that it was in this area a U.S. offensive against Japan would begin, and indeed, the U.S. Army's preparations for this were rapidly building up in Australia.

The Japanese army had captured Rabaul on the island of New Britain on January 23. Rabaul had two airfields and a good anchorage and was the best point from which to control New Guinea and the Solomons. Land-based planes of the Naval Air Corps had advanced to Rabaul as soon as it had been secured and from there launched attacks mainly on Port Moresby, New Guinea. To shut off the connection between Australian forces and U.S. forces fully, however, Imperial Headquarters came to regard the capture of New Guinea and the Solomon Islands as a priority.

Japanese forces had already captured Malaya, Burma, the Philippines, and Dutch Indonesia since the war's outbreak. Australia's importance as a base for an American counterattack had not escaped them. There were those in the navy who insisted on the capture of Australia, but the army thought such an attempt reckless. Finally it was decided to capture strong points in New Guinea and in the Solomons area. The first point to capture would be Port Moresby, the main port of New Guinea.

On July 20, an advanced party of the South Sea detached troops (commanded by Major General Tomitaro Horii) departed Rabaul and managed to land near Buna on the north shore of the immense island of New Guinea. On the night of July 28, they succeeded in defeating an Australian battalion and capturing Kokoda Airfield. The main force of the South Sea detached troops followed them and began the march to Port Moresby, crossing the steep Owen Stanley Range. Each man carried 2.4 gallons of rice, rations for a month.

Then on August 7, the war unexpectedly flared up in the Solomon Islands. To cover the advance in New Guinea, more air bases were being built in the south end of the Solomon Islands. One, a seaplane base, was on Tulagi Island. Another was on Guadalcanal Island.

At 5:30 A.M. that day, the headquarters of the Eighth Fleet (whose commander was Vice Admiral Gunichi Mikawa) at Rabaul received an emergency message from Tulagi and Guadalcanal Islands. The message said that both islands were under heavy bombardment from American ships and aircraft. The Rabaul base was thrown into confusion.

Then came another report from Tulagi. "Enemy troops from numerous ships made a surprise landing on Guadalcanal Island and Tulagi Island under the cover of powerful air corps and escort fleets. The garrison and construction troops are having a hard fight. The garrison of Tulagi resolved to make a last stand at around six."

And around noon, it was reported from Guadalcanal that American troops had landed there. The forces of the landing operation were of a fairly large scale, with one battleship, two aircraft carriers, three cruisers, fifteen destroyers, and thirty to forty transport ships. It was only nine months since the outbreak of the war and already the great counterattack of the American forces had begun.

Sixteen

Guadalcanal! The conflict centered around this small island in the Solomons revealed a weird aspect of the war between the United States and Japan. The huge creature that was the war was endlessly absorbing many lives, great numbers of ships, and other materials.

The Japanese army and navy landed many soldiers to try to recapture Guadalcanal from the 20,000 American troops that had landed on August 7. The tragedy of the dominance of materials over humans began from this time.

Though the Japanese navy sank many American ships in the First, Second, and Third Solomon or Southern Pacific sea battles, and maintained its superiority, the soldiers in Guadalcanal were overwhelmed by the great numbers of American soldiers and their superior firepower. Bravely they repeatedly tried to infiltrate and attack the American positions at night with the poor weapons they had. But the result was casualties ten times the number sustained by their enemies.

The gap between American economic strength and Japan's showed plainly at Guadalcanal. The Americans demonstrated an ability to supply themselves abundantly. It was as if a conveyor belt had been laid between the U.S. mainland and Guadalcanal.

Against this, supplies to the Japanese defenders were almost nil, reflecting Japan's poor economic position. Almost 30,000 Japanese troops were isolated into starvation and shortage of weapons. Starving, they ate reptiles and anything that moved. They even took to eating grass and tree bark. Things got so bad that Lieutenant General Haruyoshi Hyakutake, commander of the Seventeenth Army, and also commander at Guadalcanal, wrote a heart-rending report: "It is half a month since we last received supplies of rations, and with the small supply we got then, most of our troops are already suffering from malnutrition. More than 100 die of starvation a day. None among all the troops has the strength to bear an attack operation."

In these circumstances, the Eleventh Air Fleet (commanded by Vice Admiral Fumizo Tsukahara) based in Rabaul, spared no resources in a stand against the superior American air forces over Guadalcanal Island.

On August 7, while the landings were in progress, twenty-seven land-based torpedo bombers and eighteen Zeros made a sortie. They attacked the American troop transports and fought with the F4F Wildcat fighters from the carriers. They were outnumbered by several times, but even so, they managed to shoot down forty-six American planes. After that, they sallied to Guadalcanal almost every day.

The Zeros and other Japanese aircraft faced some serious obstacles in attacking Guadalcanal. One was the immense distance from Rabaul. In the transoceanic flight from Taiwan to the Philippines on the first day of the war, the Zeros successfully flew 450 nautical miles to their target. But it was 560 miles from Rabaul to Guadalcanal—over a hundred nautical miles more. Zeros could still make this journey, but because of consuming too much fuel in the air battles, many were forced to make emergency landings on the return journey.

The navy constructed the Buin step base to remove this problem. But there was a gulf of difference between the abilities of the Americans and the Japanese in building air bases. Japanese construction troops used picks and shovels and carried straw baskets naked. The Americans used bulldozers and other earthmoving machines and took little time to make an airfield. They could also repair a damaged airfield in no time with their equipment.

A further burden to the Naval Air Corps was the seemingly endless reinforcement of the U.S. Army and Air Force. The fighters from Rabaul had shot down very many American planes in spite of the great distance they had to travel. But reinforcement proceeded rapidly and the gap between the numbers of American and Japanese planes increased. Under such conditions, Zero fighters usually fought surrounded by many American fighters. Facing such swarms was hard for pilots who had to brace up their tired bodies after having flown the great distance from Rabaul.

At this time the Americans introduced new fighters. One of them was the P-38 Lightning. The Japanese had known of its existence since before the war. It was a large-size fighter, twin-engined and twin-boomed, designed and developed by the Lockheed company. Model F had a heavy armament of four sets of 12.7-millimeter machine guns and a twenty-millimeter cannon. The P-38 performed extremely well at high altitudes with its turbosupercharged engines of 3,000 horsepower. It was especially good at fast diving and fast horizontal flying because of liquid-cooled engines and high wing loading. The P-38 reminded the Japanese of a strange, huge bird with twin bodies. It was thought by the Americans to be an effective challenger of the Zero.

In battle, these two fighters made a strange sight. The Zero with its 1,000-horsepower engine was considerably smaller than the P-38. Its graceful shape looked fragile beside the menacing double-bodied American fighter. However, the hopes the Americans had of the P-38 were disappointed. The Zero's astonishing maneuverability made it seem like a shooting star around the P-38s, and it shot them down easily. The Americans were shocked. Once more it was brought home to them how difficult and dangerous it was to challenge the Zero.

As a result, the tactics devised by Major John Sati in his research on the Zero captured in the Aleutians were adopted for the P-38. The fighter was suited well to these tactics—excellent at high-altitude flying and the deep, fast dive. The Zero was deficient in these areas and therefore vulnerable. These tactics meant that the P-38 was absolutely to avoid getting into dogfights with the Zero. The P-38 was to dive from a high altitude at the Zero, and if its attack failed it was to escape, taking advantage of its high speed in climbing and horizontal flight.

These passive tactics caused no trouble to the Zero, of course. But they also made it impossible for the Zero to catch the P-38, and this was a source of irritation to the Japanese pilots. The Zero was still demonstrating its superiority over American fighters. Its existence was a great pillar of support for the numerically inferior Japanese airforce.

American medium bombers and torpedo bombers were easy targets for the Zero. Zeros encountered two-seater Douglas SBD Dauntless carrier-borne bombers, three-seater Grumman TBF carrier-borne torpedo bombers, Consolidated PBY flying boats, North American B-25s, and the Martin B-26 bombers of the army and easily shot them down.

There were U.S. aircraft, however, that even the Zero, for all its excellent performance, could not shoot down. These were the army's Boeing B-17 and the Consolidated B-24, both large, four-engine aircraft. Taking advantage of their great radius of action, 750 miles for the B-17 and 850 for the B-24, these planes could come from bases far beyond the range of even the Type 1 land-based torpedo bomber and shower great quantities of bombs from their huge bodies.

Their destructive power was awesome, and the damage they did to Japanese forces increased. Zeros took off to intercept them, but not for nothing were these big bombers called "the Flying Fortress." Both had protection against fighter bullets that was unparalleled among the world's aircraft. They could not be shot down easily. They were covered with strong armor. Their fuel tanks were self-sealing, so that even if they were punctured by twenty-millimeter cannon fire, they seldom caught fire.

The only way to damage these planes was to shoot at the crew, especially the pilot, or to strike the fuel tanks with concentrations of twenty-millimeter shells. A number of fighters swarming in attack could also inflict severe damage. But the defensive fire of these bombers was heavy. They had gun positions in the nose, the tail, above, below, and on both sides, which left no dead angle. They were not easy to approach. And pilots often miscalculated the shooting distance because of the enormous size of the airframe.

Still, in spite of these difficulties, heralded by the case of Zeros shooting down their first B-17 during the attack on Luzon Island in the Philippines right at the outbreak of the war, the Zeros kept charging these huge flying objects, trying to penetrate their heavy defensive fire.

Seventeen

The year 1943 began. The battle over Guadalcanal had already reached its final stage. The supply route to the Japanese defenders was cut off. Japanese positions were under such heavy bombardment from U.S. forces that it seemed the intention was to bury them with iron. The starved defenders had already lost most of their fighting power.

Imperial General Headquarters at last decided to abandon Guadalcanal. The evacuation started January 30. Fortunately, it was not detected by the American forces, and it ended successfully on February 7. It left behind the corpses of 15,000 killed in action and 4,500 who had died of disease, starvation, or other causes.

By the end of Guadalcanal, Japan had also lost since Pearl Harbor 893 aircraft, and 2,632 skilled air crewmen. Losses in ships had also been heavy. Such attrition was a burden greater than the Japanese forces, so poor in materials, had imagined.

The American forces' counterattack was rapidly taking form. After capturing Guadalcanal Island, they secured a base in the New Guinea area. They completely destroyed the Japanese troops at Buna and approached Lae and Salamaua.

The Naval Air Corps, mainly based at Rabaul, put up a desperate fight. But the gap between the means of the Americans and Japanese widened more and more. It was in these circumstances that the Battle of the Bismarck Sea occurred. The Japanese tried to reinforce Lae and Salamaua. They sent about 100 army and navy fighters to escort their convoy, but the effort ended in miserable defeat. Almost 4,000 soldiers and almost all the ships were lost and twenty to thirty Zero fighters shot down.

The Imperial Headquarters, upset by the worsening status of the war, ordered operation "I Go" to try to regain the initiative in the war. Only the air force was to be used. The intention of I Go was to carry out air raids on a large scale against both the Solomon Islands and New Guinea, using all of the Naval Air Corps. The attack force consisted of 182 fighters, eighty-one bombers, seventy-two land-based torpedo bombers, and four reconnaissance planes—339 aircraft in total. Admiral Isoroku Yamamoto, commander in chief of the combined fleet, left his flagship, the giant battleship *Musashi,* at Truk Island, and came to Rabaul to command the operation directly.

The operation began on April 7, 1943. Sorties were carried out on April 11, 12, and 14, and sank one cruiser, one destroyer, and thirty-five transports. One hundred eighty-three aircraft were shot down, while the damage to the Japanese side came to forty-two aircraft self-destroyed or missing. Operation I Go ended on April 16. Next day, a study conference on the operation began in the presence of Admiral Yamamoto.

Many members of the naval air force were in attendance, and there were serious discussions about the problems of the aerial war. The first conclusion of the conference was to reconfirm that "the Zero fighter is excellent in overall performances. It is by no means inferior to any American fighter that has appeared in the south east area to the present." Upon this premise, frank opinions were exchanged.

From analysis of the U.S. Air Force at that time, it was clear that the Americans were committing their best fighters to the New Guinea and Solomon Islands area. These were the Grumman F4F, the Chance Vought F4U Corsair, the Lockheed P-38 Lightning, the Bell P-39 Airacobra and the Curtiss P-40 Tomahawk. Of all these aircraft, the performances of the newly appearing F4U were specially noted.

The F4U was a naval fighter. The Japanese believed that it could not be used on carriers because of its poor deck landing performance (it had a tendency to bounce—soon fixed) and poor visibility. But as it had been deployed at Guadalcanal and other land bases, the F4U had been able to bring its full capabilities into play.

The F4U was the first single-engine fighter equipped with an air-cooled, 2,000-horsepower engine. It was superior to the Zero in horizontal speed and climbing rate, and it had an especially high diving speed. It also performed well at high altitudes. It was obviously the best fighter the Americans had to place against the Zero. Even with these abilities, however, the F4U could not fight evenly against the Zero in dogfighting, and only after the Americans had adopted special tactics against the Zero did it become difficult for Zeros to shoot them down.

These tactics were that if the situation became unfavorable, the F4U would climb to a height of 8,000 or 9,000 meters. At these altitudes, the Zero was an inferior performer.

While their numbers were small, the F4Us caused no trouble. But as their numbers rapidly increased, it often happened that they could make an attack from all directions. It became impossible to ignore this new fighter. The conference had to admit that at last an American fighter able to match the Zero had appeared.

There was also one other remarkable conclusion at the conference. It was that "in the future, protection should be considered even for fighters."

Aircraft were downed mostly by catching fire. The damage could be lessened if the defensive strength was increased, especially protection from bullets. However, in the Japanese army and navy, the belief was that offense was the best defense, and therefore, the requirements of the offense dominated. Thus, to lessen the weight of the plane even by a gram, bullet protection was not required. Defense was neglected to increase the offensive performance. This idea was applied even to large and slow bombers, which could not escape gunfire in an encounter with fighters.

The Zero, of course, had no bullet protection. After meeting all the requirements for an all-purpose fighter with a small engine of only 1,000 horsepower, the Zero had no room left for protection. But since the start of the war, it had become obvious that the Type 1 land-based torpedo bomber was too vulnerable to bullets. As a result, its activities had to be restricted to night flight, and in the day it had to be fully escorted by fighters. This was how serious the lack of bullet protection had become for the Type 1 land-based torpedo bomber. It was proof that bullet protection for the Zero was of secondary importance that such protection was only coming up for serious consideration one year after the war had started.

Anyway, the Zero was still showing that it had the best fighting ability among Japanese and American fighters two years and eight months after its debut in the war in China. This was very rare in the world of aviation, which was distinguished by a dazzling rate of progress and change, accelerated yet more by war.

The study conference produced much valuable information by its end. It was agreed that this information should be implemented in the air force in the future.

Operation I Go had ended. Yamamoto was scheduled to inspect front line bases at Ballale, Shortlands, and Buin with his staff on the eighteenth of April, and on the nineteenth to leave Rabaul and return to the *Musashi* at Truk. However, the coded telegram giving notice of the inspection had been picked up and decoded by the Americans and sent to Henderson Field on Guadalcanal Island by classified telegram. Those at the field became mad with joy and prepared to intercept Yamamoto's plane.

On April 18, in the morning, the head officers of the combined fleet, including Admiral Yamamoto, boarded two Type 1 land-based torpedo bombers and took off from Rabaul escorted by six Zero fighters. When they got above Buin at 7:40 A.M., they were suddenly attacked by sixteen American fighters lying in wait. The attackers were P-38s of Henderson Field's 339 Squadron commanded by Major John Mitchell.

Instantly a violent air battle erupted between the Zeros and the twin-engined, twin-boomed P-38s. The Type 1 torpedo bombers attempted to escape at low altitudes, but the one carrying Admiral Yamamoto was hit and caught fire. It crashed into the jungle at a low angle, eleven nautical miles west of Buin. The second bomber carrying Ugaki, chief of the general staff of the combined fleet, and other officers went down into the sea south of Cape Moila.

The Zero fighters, inferior in number to their attackers, could not protect the two bombers. So Yamamoto and many of his staff died.

The death of Admiral Isoroku Yamamoto, commander in chief of the combined fleet and a pioneer in the principal of naval air power, was a grievous shock to the Naval Air Corps at Rabaul. It was a loss sad enough to cancel out the success of I Go.

However, there was no time for sentiment. The American forces were steadily capturing islands, one by one. They were clearly intending to surround and isolate Rabaul, the most important front-line base for Japanese control of the Solomons and the securing of New Guinea. In the Solomons, a naval force under Admiral Halsey and in New Guinea combined American-Australian land forces under General Douglas MacArthur dominated the Japanese army troops under Major General Tomitaro Horii.

The Japanese troops, repeatedly bombed by many aircraft, defended a landscape of craters. They also had no supplies. They faced starvation while above them the huge B-24s and B-17s raided, escorted by many fighters. Zeros challenged them, though outnumbered. They looked like tragic heroes, keeping up their attacks against great odds and with little logistical support from Japan's poor industrial strength.

While these hard battles were being fought, suddenly on May 12, more than 20,000 American troops landed on Attu Island in the Aleutian Islands. A stiff battle with the more than 2,000 Japanese defenders began.

With no reinforcements, the Japanese resisted under continuous fire and bombing from above. Their position soon became hopeless, and on May 29, about two weeks after the landing on Attu, they sent a message announcing their intention to be completely annihilated, rather than surrender: "All left are about to sally forth." In the end, 2,300 died on Attu. Only twenty-nine prisoners were taken. Most of them were too severely wounded to control their actions. Others, wounded, killed themselves rather than be captured.

The fall of Attu and the retreat from Kiska Island meant that a new defense of the northern approaches to Japan had to be developed quickly. The navy spared planes for bases on the Kurile Islands and Hokkaido. Just at that time, its air forces in the southeastern Pacific descended to a new level of inferiority.

In New Guinea, U.S. and Australian troops under General Douglas MacArthur kept up their advance. An amphibious attack on the Solomons with many troops by a naval force under Admiral Halsey was also rapidly developing. The tactics of this attack were to destroy utterly the defenses of the Japanese troops by thorough and repeated bombing. Then, under cover of an immense bombardment by ships and planes, many troops landed, and with their plentiful weapons, destroyed the Japanese troops. Immediately after, construction troops came ashore and built an airfield in short order using large earth moving machines. In this way, with their rich supply of materials and mechanization, the Americans captured the Solomons one by one.

Their tactics were very effective. The Japanese retreated along the Solomon Islands until at last they only had Bougainville Island.

The Americans finally started a landing operation there on the morning of November 1. Admiral Mineichi Koga, the new commander in chief of the combined fleet, judged that the Japanese had a good chance of demolishing American sea power if he attacked the operation with all the naval power left. He concentrated many ships and advanced 167 aircraft to Rabaul Base. These included eighty-two Zeros of the First Air Group. With this reinforced air force of 773 aircraft, 370 of which were operable, Koga tried to improve the declining war situation with one blow.

The operation, called "Ro Go" was carried out on the first, fifth, eighth, eleventh, thirteenth, and seventeenth of November. But in spite of the navy's expectations, they did not get the desired results. On the contrary, the Japanese troops were almost annihilated. As for the naval air force, they shot down many U.S. Army and Navy planes, but lost 200 precious aircraft themselves.

The failure of this operation put the Naval Air Corps into a tight corner. An American air base on Bougainville was quickly built and from there B-17s and B-24s started to continuously raid the base, dropping enormous quantities of bombs. Rabaul began losing its capability to be an air base.

Eighteen

---

*B*y the end of 1943, the number of workers at the Nagoya Aircraft Works had grown to 43,000, and the area of the factory had expanded to 221,000 *tsubo*. In 1943, the Nagoya works factory produced and sent to the battlefield 1,029 Zeros, the Nakajima Aircraft Company 1,967. But demands for increases in production, even by one, became more and more severe from the army and navy.

The military demands did not take the production capability of the factory into consideration, and they were forced upon the Nagoya works and other aircraft companies. The Nagoya works spared no effort to try to increase production. But there was a limit to what could be done. In 1941, the year previous to the start of the war, production had remained at 1,697, about 80 percent of the 2,038 planes wanted by the army and navy. In the next year, 1942, the production of 2,514 aircraft had been 75 percent of the military's requirement for 3,287 aircraft. One of the main factors that had prevented an increase in production was the armed forces' many requests for improvements to aircraft under production.

The Zero especially was the object of frequent requests for improvements. Requests from the battlefields led the Zero to be changed from the Model II to the Model 21, the Model 22, the Model 52, the

Model 52-Ko, and the Model 52-Otsu. Then came the Model 52-Hei, the Model 63 and the Model 54-Hei. There were many model changes by the end of the war.

These requests for improvements indicated how great were the expectations the navy had of the Zero. But the process of designing, manufacturing, and testing these changes took a lot of trouble. Making these changes was one of the reasons the Nagoya works lagged behind Nakajima in turning out planes.

An increase in production was also prevented by shifts in demand from the navy. An order to decrease the production of Zeros in favor of the Raiden interceptor was later changed back to an increase in Zeros, because of the Raiden's low popularity in the navy. The navy couldn't be blamed for these rapid changes in production orders, but they caused difficulty on the production line and made smooth production almost impossible. Still, the engineers and workers spared no effort to obey the orders of the armed forces.

One of the results of this situation was a method of increasing production called the advancing working steps. It was developed by three engineers, Wataru Sasaki, Morito Doi, and Minoru Ishii of the second manufacturing section for the production of army aircraft.

The advancing steps production method was a kind of assembly line system in which the assembly of the airframe was divided into steps. At timed intervals, the airframes under construction were moved to the next construction stage at the sound of a bugle. This meant the workers had to finish an assembly stage within a given period. The completely assembled airframe was carried out of the factory with the ceremony of hoisting the Rising Sun flag. Watching workers took off their caps.

This method not only increased production, it also made it possible to plan for production. It was adopted by the first manufacturing section for the production of naval planes and then by other munitions factories. The three engineers who had devised the three step system received an unusual army commendation for a distinguished technical contribution from the prime minister and General Tojo, the war minister.

The government was also desperately trying to increase the production of munitions. As part of this effort, Ginjiro Fujiwara, a cabinet adviser who was also a member of the Mitsui business cartel, was asked to do a political survey of the munitions industry. Fujiwara enthusiastically went round the munitions factories, pointing out the proper methods to be adopted in order to ensure production increases. He came round to the Nagoya works in September 1943.

Fujiwara planned to triple the production of aircraft in 1944, and with this supposition, he began to survey all the sections of the works. In the course of this, Fujiwara noticed how the planes were being transported.

They were still being taken by oxcart to Kagamigahara Airfield, a journey taking twenty-four hours. But the oxen were becoming severely exhausted. And their feed, obtained on the black market, was at last becoming difficult to get. As a result, the number of useless animals was increasing. The works had had fifty oxen at the start of the war. Now they had thirty. Meanwhile, the production of aircraft was increasing. The transport by oxcarts could not keep up. To help out, transport of aircraft by water was started to the Nagoya International Airfield in the Minato ward on the opposite shore within Nagoya.

Of the aircraft constructed at the Nagoya works, small ones were not a problem to transport by oxcart. But large ones presented extreme difficulty. At first, large planes also travelled by oxcart to Kagamigahara, but in the town of Komaki there was a right-angle corner among the houses to be turned. The fuselages of the big planes were too long for it, and to get them through it was necessary to lift both carts and fuselage and slowly make the turn. Damage occurred sometimes, with airframes touching eaves, bending roofs and electrical poles. This method could not be used for very large planes.

Then, before the Nagoya International Field was constructed, those in charge of transportation were ordered to transport the army's Type 22 super-heavy bombers—a modification of the Junkers G-38 transport.

The Type 22 bomber was a four-engine plane of no significant performances. Mitsubishi produced six in total—two in 1930, two in 1932, and one each in 1933 and 1935. Further production was canceled after that. Still, they had to be transported to the airfield, or they could not fly.

The fuselage of the plane was divided in two parts so that three oxcarts could transport them and the tail wings. But the main wings were so huge, oxcarts could not be used. Seiichiro Tamura, the transportation supervisor, was astonished at the sight of these wings. He went over every transport method imaginable with his superiors, and at last came to the conclusion that there was no other way except to sail up the Kiso River from the sea and land the wings near the Kagamigahara Airfield about sixty kilometers from the river mouth. The wings would then have to be carried to the airfield by land. It was an extraordinary transportation method, far from what usually made sense. But there was no other way.

Tamura had the Onishi company prepare a large barge at the seashore in back of the works and loaded it with the main wings. The barge sailed up the coast for Ise Bay towed by a steamboat, then sailed up the Kiso River. After seven hours it reached Kasamatsu, forty kilometers from the mouth of the river. From there, the river turned right and its narrow width and sharp curves became difficult to navigate. It also became shallow. Immediately, the barge touched bottom.

Tamura and Sokichi Onishi, the head of the Onishi company, had anticipated this. They stopped the tow boat and attached two thick ropes to the barge and made laborers on shore pull the ropes to their shouts. Meanwhile, people from the villages along the shore gathered in curiosity. It was the first time they had ever seen a big ship in this part of the river. Tamura gathered another 200 laborers from the villages headed by the local riverboat skippers Shohachi Kawada and Mineichi and Choichi Noda, brothers from Kawashima village. They insisted that it was impossible for a vessel so big to sail up to Kagamigahara, especially loaded with the airplane.

"Don't say nothing!" Tamura replied in a hard tone. "Even if we have to use our own hands, we have to carry them. Those who are willing, come with us!"

Kawada and the others were impressed by Tamura's strong spirit and promised their cooperation. They tackled the enormous barge along with the laborers of the Onishi company.

The barge had buried itself in the riverbed. The laborers dug out the gravel and stones with shovels and carried them ashore. And when the channel had been made deep enough, with shouts those on shore hauled once more on the ropes to the signal of a blue flag swung by the foreman.

In this way the barge advanced a few meters, rubbing the bottom. Then it buried itself in the riverbed again. Again the laborers jumped into the water with their shovels and set to deepening the bed. The sun set while they repeated this work. It was only sixteen kilometers from Kasamatsu to the village of Koyamawatari where the landing was scheduled. Still, it took four days to go that far.

Once landed, the outer wings still had to be carried to Kagamigahara, four kilometers away. As there was no road, the wings had to be pushed on plates laid on the ground. But progress was blocked by a big pine forest behind the landing spot. Tamura opened negotiations with the landowner and got permission to cut down pines. One by one they were cut down until at last the wings emerged from the forest and crossed some sweet potato fields. They also crossed the bank, and finally they reached a corner of Kagamigahara Airfield. It had taken two days to cover that four kilometers.

This was how the outer wings of six Type 92 heavy bombers and the fuselages of ten Type 1 land-based torpedo bombers in trial production were carried to Kagamigahara Airfield. But after the Nagoya International Field was constructed, the large planes were taken there mainly by water.

Transportation to Nagoya International Field by water was started in 1943. Airframes were loaded on a barge at the southern wharf on a site adjacent to the works. The loading and unloading of the barge was difficult, except at high tide, so the time of transport became tied to the high tide time, regardless of whether that came in the day or night.

It took about forty minutes to reach Nagoya International Airfield. Two barges were used at a time. A load of five Zeros or one Type 1 torpedo bomber could be carried. It was an effective method of transportation; the greatest danger was waves. The freeboard of the barge was only thirty centimeters—so low that even a small wave could sink it. Since the load was military planes, a loss would have been serious. Those in charge of transportation devoted themselves to the task of fighting the waves.

Except for large airframes, however, the main method of transportation remained land transport to Kagamigahara by oxcart. With a car Fujiwara spent a week looking over the oxcart transport system. He was astonished at what he saw and immediately came up with recommendations. The first was that the oxen had to have an ample supply of feed. Then he wanted automobiles to be fitted for transporting the planes, and consideration given to transportation by railroad. At last, there looked to be signs of improvement to the transport system with oxcarts.

Fujiwara asked the armed forces for the loan of automobiles and a supply of gasoline and he requested the cooperation of the Ministry of Railways in obtaining railway transport.

For the automobile transport, twenty tractors with trailers were lent by the Takakura Army Yard by order of Lieutenant General Mitsugu Okada, the commander of the Eastern Shore Forces. But the bad road conditions could not be overcome with these. The trailers rolled and bounced violently. When the planes reached Kagamigahara, cracks were found on the underside of the fuselages. The tractors tried reducing speed, but such was the road, cracking of the fuselages was not prevented even then. Finally, the tractors had to be given up.

Transport by railroad was tried next. Twenty officials, including Inspector Ozawa, came from the Ministry of Railways to look over the situation. As a result they decided to attempt railway transportation using twelve large open freight cars from the Oe area, where the Nagoya works was situated, to Kagamigahara Airfield.

Railroad transportation was thought to be effective, especially for large planes. Transport by barge was working, but production was increasing, and soon the barges would not be able to keep up. There were also continuing worries about wind and wave conditions. The railway seemed better.

Seiichiro Tamura, the transportation supervisor, made his men look into how best to do the railway transport. The first problem was the size of the open car. Even a large-size open freight car was too small to carry the aircraft. The small fuselage of a fighter could be put obliquely on the car, but a large fuselage projected over considerably. There were tunnels along the way. And if the fuselage touched signal poles and other trackside structures, it would be badly damaged.

Tamura discussed his findings with the Ministry of Railways and lowered the floor of the freight cars. He also walked the tunnels on foot. Finally he was confident. The first train of open freight cars started. Tamura boarded an open freight car with its load. The car shook violently and the airframe was swinging from left to right. Tamura was seized with uneasiness.

His uneasiness deepened in a dark tunnel. The slightest touch with the wall and the airframe would shift from its calculated position and might jam. That would destroy the other frames following behind. The tunnel would fill with scattered pieces of duralumin. As the train rumbled through the tunnel, Tamura had no thought for his own life.

He only prayed and hoped as transportation supervisor that no damage would occur to these planes, so badly needed on the battlefield.

At last the cargo train emerged from the tunnel. Under the bright sunshine, Tamura felt a deep relief and then something hot coming out of his heart. He kept rocking on the car, his face down, and not bothering to wipe the tears falling down his cheeks.

However, transport by railway soon reached its limits. Five open freight cars were necessary to carry one large bomber. The largest army planes under construction at the Nagoya works then was the Type 97 heavy bomber. Twelve open freight cars were not enough to cover all the production of this plane. Then came a change in the situation which made railway transportation impossible: the Type 4 heavy bomber Hiryu (code name: Peggy) came into mass production instead of the Type 97 heavy bomber.

The Type 4 heavy bomber was the army's twin-engined bomber. It had been developed at the Nagoya works by the team of Teruo Tojo, Iwane Murakami, Bin Saito, Shigeru Ueki, and other design engineers headed by chief designer Hisanojo Ozawa. It was inferior to the Type 1 land-based torpedo bomber in its range, but among the twin-engined bombers of the army and navy, it was distinguished for its speed, maneuverability, and heavy defensive armament.

The transport of this plane troubled Tamura and others, however. The Type 4 was a very big plane, its main wings were much bigger than those of the Type 97 heavy bomber. It could not be loaded on freight cars. That brought the use of automobiles and trains, recommended by Fujiwara, to an end. What was left was transportation by barge or—oxcart.

But the oxen had gradually become exhausted and increases in production only made conditions worse for the animals. There was also great competition for draught animals from the many other munitions factories in the south part of Nagoya. It was becoming difficult to get new ones. Automobiles could have been used if a new road had been constructed. But labor and materials were scarce and anyway, at least at first, no one considered a new road seriously.

At the end of November, the troops defending Tarawa and the Makin Islands were annihilated. The American counterattack went on building. In Europe, Germany suffered a major setback at Stalingrad. Italy surrendered unconditionally to the Allies after the fall of Mussolini. The world situation for Japan was becoming worse and worse.

Nineteen

The year 1944 started with a raid by American forces on the Marshall Islands. Japanese troops defending Kwajalein Island and Eniwetok Atoll were destroyed. Large scale air raids were carried out repeatedly against Truk Island, the most important base of the Japanese defense line.

Air raids on Truk caused the immense loss of forty-three ships and 271 planes to the Japanese. Truk ceased to be a naval base, and this caused a major retreat of the line of defense. Rabaul, the Naval Air Corps base, became isolated and lost its strategic value.

For this reason, Mineichi Koga, the commander in chief of the combined fleet, ordered a general retreat of the forces in Rabaul. That meant the end of fighting for the Solomon Islands from Rabaul.

One year of ferocious fighting had caused terrific damage to the Japanese side. Tremendous numbers of aircraft, 6,000 of the navy's and 2,000 of the army's, had been committed to the area round Rabaul. They had shot down or destroyed large numbers of American aircraft. But the Japanese army and navy had lost nearly all of those 8,000 planes they had committed. In addition, the army had lost 90,000 and the navy 40,000 in action. Seventy fighting ships and 115 merchant vessels had been lost. The Solomon Islands had turned out to be a great graveyard.

In Rabaul, a garrison of about 75,000 army personnel and 40,000 navy were left. All the aircraft were to retreat except a few sea planes. The maintenance crews of the aircraft were left without defending troops.

One by one, the aircraft left Rabaul Base. Among them the Zeros went down the runway, their faded paint work dimly shining. They took off and their landing gear retracted as if embracing. Ground crews waved their caps and hands. The aircraft circled above and then headed away. The aircrews leaving and the ground crews being left behind wept.

The loss of so many aircraft was also the loss of skilled pilots. This caused a decrease in the quality of the aircrews. After the retreat from Rabaul, the Japanese forces began to show signs of decline.

Early in 1944, Mizushima Aircraft Works in Okayama, a sub-factory of the Nagoya Aircraft Works, started operations. Kumamoto works also reached operational stage. The Zero fighter was being produced at the rate of 100-odd a month at the Nagoya works and at about 200 a month at the Nakajima Aircraft Company.

The spirit of the Nagoya works was unusually high. The number of new workers increased rapidly. The factory was crowded with people. The newly adopted workers were assigned to the production line after logging one month of practice training. Their skill was of course low, so the experienced workers had to guide them, even leaving their duties to do so. This produced the risk of lowering the quality of the aircraft produced. Still, engineers and workers kept on driving their tired bodies. The production numbers rose steadily.

The increase in production made the problem of transportation more serious. Yasujiro Okano, the director of the works had worried about this problem. He consulted the vice president of Mitsubishi, Hikoyata Iwasaki, who had happened to come to the works (Iwasaki's family had founded the Mitsubishi financial combine). Okano and Iwasaki followed the slow moving train of oxcarts by car as far as the edge of Nagoya. Iwasaki heard from Okano why oxcarts were being used, and that the oxen were exhausted. Ox transportation had come to its limit and could not keep up with increases in production.

"How about horses?" Iwasaki said, annoyed by the slowness of the oxen.

Okano explained that with horses there was a risk of stampede. It had also sometimes happened that the airframes they were transporting hit utility poles and houses and were damaged. Horses also had the disadvantage of a stamina inferior to oxen. But the main reason for not using horses was that it was a scramble with everyone else to get them. Horses were hardly obtainable in the Nagoya area.

Iwasaki, however, was good at riding, and the Iwasaki family had some horse farms of its own. He said he would consider the horse problem and see if he could make use of his family's horse farms to help solve the problem.

After a few days, two sunburned men came to the Nagoya works. They were the brothers Masao and Takujiro Dewa, manager of the Iwasaki horse farms in Chiba Prefecture and Hokkaido. Director Okano introduced the Dewa brothers to Seiichiro Tamura, who had been promoted to chief of the transportation section. With straw sandals on their feet, the Dewa brothers then followed at night the train of oxcarts to Kagamigahara Airfield.

The Dewas were surprised to see modern aircraft factories relying on oxen to move their airframes and for a short time kept their silence even after they had arrived at Kagamigahara Airfield. Then they simultaneously uttered the word: "Percheron."

"What is that?" Tamura asked, puzzled.

"It's a kind of horse," Takujiro said. "There is a kind of horse called Percheron. That kind of horse is calm and never stampedes. They have enormous strength and are patient. The efficiency of transport will surely increase if you use them," he concluded in a decisive tone.

Tamura talked of this with Director Okano and the Dewa brothers. Okano agreed at once. He decided to buy Percherons and made the Dewa brothers part-time employees of the transportation section. They were entrusted with the purchase of the horses.

The Dewa brothers went to Chiba, Yamagata, Morioka, Iwate, and Hokkaido searching for Percherons. Then came a report to the transportation section that horses had arrived at Atsuta station. With members of his section Tamura went there to receive them. He was amazed at the sight of the horses in the freight car. They were strange, bigger than any horse he had seen, with stout frames and unusually long hair growing thickly on their legs.

Tamura had his men guide the ten odd horses through the main street. Every passerby, it seemed, could not help stopping to stare in amazement. Soon the train of horses entered the gate of the Nagoya Aircraft Works.

After one day's rest, the transportation of airframes with the horses started. On that day, Tamura went along with his men to Kagamigahara to see how the horses did. The workers were extremely pleased with the ability of the animals. They easily towed the carts to the airfield, almost without rest. It had taken twenty-four hours to reach Kagamigahara with oxen. With Percherons, the journey took twelve, half the previous time. The horses were also extremely gentle. They gave no sign of being startled when an automobile horn sounded close by. The Percherons solved the problem of transportation.

However, the American offensive in the Pacific was increasing in scale. The battlefield moved to the central Pacific. Their target now became Saipan Island in the Marianas. The island was attacked heavily from the air and a bombardment by more than forty ships including eight battleships started. On June 15, the first wave of up to 120 landing craft headed for the island, launched from transports that covered the ocean. The Marianas were an important area for the defense of the Japanese mainland. The army and navy tried to cooperate in an operation to destroy the U.S. task force.

This operation was called A-Go and started with the landing of the Americans on Saipan Island. The Japanese navy would commit all its ships in this operation and in a single blow retrieve the declining situation. But the results were miserable. The air force especially received heavy damage and was almost destroyed. Many aircraft in the battle were from the three large aircraft carriers and six converted carriers, escorted by forty-six ships including the *Yamato* and *Musashi*. But in the repeated attacks of American planes launched from their task forces, the Japanese carriers *Taiho* (the flagship) and *Shokaku* and *Hiyo* were sunk, and other ships were also heavily damaged. All except twenty-five of the aircraft from the carriers were shot down or destroyed. The air crews of the carrier-borne craft were highly trained and their loss in such numbers was extremely serious for the Naval Air Corps.

For this battle, many aircraft had been positioned at bases in the Marianas to join in Operation A-Go. But they were struck first by the American air forces and most were lost. The defense line that guarded the Japanese mainland was now broken, just at a time when the Naval Air Corps had been almost fatally damaged.

Many Zeros joined in the battle. But by now, the Zero's mystery had faded. American fighters had become thoroughly practiced in anti-Zero tactics. Several would attack one Zero together. And at last the Americans had come up with a fighter that was easily the Zero's match.

The new fighter was the Grumman F6F Hellcat, a big fighter equipped with an engine with more than twice the horsepower of the Zero's. It was equipped with six 12.7-millimeter machine guns and superior in bullet protection and diving speed to the Zero. It was only inferior to the Zero in its range and turning performance. At dog-fighting, the Hellcat was not better, either, being able to follow barely a quarter of the circle made by a Zero if it made a climbing turn. Then the F6F had no choice but to dive and escape. The F6F then continued the old anti-Zero tactics—diving in pairs to pour in bullets and then escaping. Dogfighting with a Zero was to be avoided.

However, the rate of being shot down for the Zero fighter was increasing. They lacked the armor protection and often the skilled pilots necessary to survive the heavy odds brought against them by the numerous, fast, and well-armed F6Fs. The time had already come when the Zero should have stepped down from its position as the main fighter and given way to a new fighter. U.S. fighters had had many successors since the war started. Japan should have gone the same way, but the navy chose to drive hard only in making many modifications to the Zero. They did that because they could not afford a successor, owing to the rapid decline of the war situation and poor industrial strength. Four years had passed since the Zero had made its debut in China. Now, there was a shadow of lonesomeness around the Zero.

Saipan Island was cut off by the failure of operation A-Go and had fallen into the hands of the Americans by July 7. After the island's commandant, Vice Admiral Chuichi Nagumo, and Lieutenant General Yoshitsugu Saito killed themselves, the 3,000 soldiers remaining sallied out in a last charge. Those left, the wounded, nurses, and many others chose suicide.

The loss of Saipan was a serious blow to Japan. America would quickly build great airfields and from there, B-29 bombers, taking advantage of their superior range, would begin a thorough bombing of the Japanese mainland. For these reasons, the Imperial General Headquarters seriously considered how to recapture Saipan. But the army and navy did not have the power left to make that possible, since superiority at sea and in the sky had been lost.

After the fall of Saipan, the garrisons of Guam and Tenian islands were destroyed. In Japan, the Tojo cabinet, which had been leading the war, resigned in a body. In Europe, German forces stood alone before the full-scale counterattack of the Allies.

Twenty

The summer of 1944 had gone, and the winds of autumn began to blow.

At the Nagoya Aircraft Works, the number of workers had been greatly increased by the inclusion of women volunteers and students to work alongside the drafted workers. But since that time a serious problem had emerged: parts could not be gotten easily.

Each factory prepared parts in accordance with the military's monthly production requirements. However, some parts from factories in the works or from subcontractors would not arrive until ten days later. Gradually this delay grew until it became twenty days before all the parts were ready for assembly. That left only ten days to complete a month's production quota for aircraft. In that time, workers worked madly to make the quota. Eventually, they were forced to overwork. It became usual for the day to start at 7 A.M. and work to go on until midnight. With such hours, workers slept together in the drill hall and other places. They seldom returned home.

Besides the lack of manufacturing machines and parts necessary for the production of aircraft, the shortage of all necessities for living became significant. Food was a priority, but there was not enough to support such hard work.

Workers devoted themselves to aircraft production without rest. Mitsubishi produced 100 Zeros in June 1944, 115 in July, 135 in both August and September, and reached a maximum of 145 in October. This was a kind of miracle, considering the shortage of parts and the worsening working conditions.

Meanwhile, Percheron horses were transporting the finished fuselages. They towed the carts day and night without rest. Their ability was impressive, and almost eighty Percherons were purchased by the works.

Then an unexpected incident occurred concerning the purchase of the horses. The Percherons had been bought with the cooperation of the Dewa brothers and Eigoro Ishizuka, the chief horse breeder of the Koiwai farm, and with the approval of Tsutomu Ashizawa and Yoshiro Kuryuzawa, horse control officials of the Iwate Prefectural government. The trouble was that the price paid for the horses broke official price regulations.

The official price for a cart horse was fixed at from 900 yen to 1,200 yen. But the Dewa brothers had paid 2,000 to 3,800 yen to get excellent horses. This raised the protest of a local horse merchant, and with secret information about these deals, he launched a law suit at the local court houses of Morioka and Hokkaido.

The Nagoya Aircraft Works was troubled by this unexpected court matter. It made a petition to the local military and employed a powerful team of defense counsels, consisting of Somei Uzawa, president of Meiji University, and Yoshio Suzuki, Fumio Takashima, and Yuzo Kudo. Mitsubishi was all prepared to win the case.

The court opened at Morioka and Hokkaido. It was a small incident, yet the court was filled with a strange tension. The charge was breaking official price regulations set by the national mobilization orders. Wrongdoing was obvious and there was no room for discussion. But since the wrongdoing had been performed under the pressure of having to produce aircraft under orders, as a matter of wartime national emergency, Mitsubishi supposed that military pressure could be applied to the judges. The case also had to be kept closed to the public, since classified information about the aircraft factories would have to be mentioned.

The Dewa brothers stated: "Witnessing at Nagoya that the swiftest military aircraft were transported on very slow oxcarts and hearing that the number of oxen was small and that they were having troubles with transportation, we worried if we could win the war in those conditions. As nationalists, we decided to help the country. And so we devoted ourselves seriously to the purchase of Percheron horses. We explained the situation and asked the officials of the prefecture for their cooperation."

The defense counsel asked harshly for a verdict of innocent, from the standpoint of national interest.

However, the court decided against Mitsubishi's expectations. The judge stated that there was no room for the excuse that the purchase of Percheron horses had no official permission from the army and declared all accused guilty. Yoshiro Kuryuzawa, the clerk of the horse control section in Iwate Prefecture who had contributed most to the purchases, was sentenced to one year in prison on the grounds that a government official could not break regulations. Takujiro Dewa and Tsutomu Ashizawa, a scientist at the horse control section of Iwate Prefectural government, were given six months, with a stay of execution for two years. Masao Dewa was fined 5,000 yen and Eigoro Ishizuka 3,000 yen.

As a result of this court case, the purchase of Percheron horses stopped at eighty-nine instead of the planned 100. The horses went on carrying airframes to Kagamigahara.

The war by now was approaching its final stage. The Japanese forces in Burma suffered a crushing defeat. In the Pacific area, the Japanese garrisons in Pelcieu Island and Morotai Island were annihilated. Then, on October 21, 1944, American troops began landing on Leyte in the Philippines from 600 ships.

Against them, the Japanese navy ordered the start of operation Sho-No-1 and concentrated all its power off Leyte. Seven battleships, including the huge *Yamato* and *Musashi,* four aircraft carriers, two hybrid battleship-carriers, fourteen heavy cruisers, seven light cruisers, and thirty-three destroyers were committed to the battle. The American navy opposed this attack with twelve battleships, twelve aircraft carriers, eighteen escort carriers, seven heavy cruisers, thirteen light cruisers, ninety-three destroyers and eleven destroyer-escorts. The battle between sixty-seven fighting ships of the Japanese navy and 166 of the U.S. Navy spread over a vast area of sea and air and was the greatest naval battle in history. The Japanese navy attacked, risking annihilation.

But the Americans were greatly superior both on the sea and in the air. The dominance of their air forces was especially responsible for victory. Exposed to the attacks of submarines and swarming American planes, the Japanese lost two battleships, including *Musashi,* four aircraft carriers, six heavy cruisers, two light cruisers, and twelve destroyers—in all twenty-seven ships, before they could catch the American ships.

With this defeat, the Japanese navy had lost half its remaining forces. It was during this operation that the Special Attack Force, which had never been seen in history, made its first sortie.

As the war went against them—from exactly when no one is sure—there rose among the members of the Japanese navy the desperate opinion that the only way to defeat the Americans so greatly superior in the quantity and quality of their arms was to send pilots on suicide missions.

Already in April 1943, more than a year past, one army fighter of the Sixth Flying Division had made a suicide attack on a B-17 and brought it down. At the end of May 1944 four army fighters under the command of Major Katsushige Takada voluntarily crashed into American ships off the southern shore of Biak Island and sank them. On October 15, Rear Admiral Masabumi Arima, the commander of the Twenty-sixth Air Flotilla, while leading eighty-seven aircraft, dove his own plane into an American task force. Arima was known to be strongly in favor of suicide attacks.

The news of these heroic crash attacks had spread to all the forces. The feeling the crash attacker, while certain to be killed, would also surely kill, became strong among the air corps of the front line. Imperial General Headquarters began to think of this as a special method of attack.

In this situation, on October 19, Vice Admiral Takijiro Onishi, who had just assumed command of the First Air Fleet, visited the base of the 201st Air Group (a fighter group) at Mabalacat in the Philippines.

With a stiff face he said to the leaders of the group: "Japan is in a most serious crisis. This Sho-No-1 operation is the last chance to escape the crisis. I repeatedly considered ways to win this operation and came to this conclusion. There is no way but the suicidal crash attack. I would like to leave this to your task group. Arm Zero fighters with bombs and make them crash into the enemy."

At this unexpected statement, the atmosphere in the room became very tense. The leaders of the fighter group closed their mouths tightly. Only their eyes flashed strangely. The grave silence continued for a long time. Then Commander Asaichi Tamai, the executive officer of the 201st Air Group, said: "Please give us a little time."

He went to the other room with Lieutenant Masanobu Ibusuki, the senior squadron leader, and consulted with him. In no time, Tamai came back and answered with a tense face: "We agree with the opinion of the commander."

Onishi simply nodded without a word.

At once the formation of the Special Attack Corps was started. Tamai called twenty-seven young pilots he had trained himself and with grief on his face explained that the Special Attack Force was necessary. He asked for volunteers. Even before his words had ended, their hands were raised as in competition. Tamai felt his breast become hot. He kept on gazing at their faces, without words.

Commander Tamai and Rikihei Inoguchi, a staff officer of the First Air Fleet, discussed the choice of a leader. Finally they agreed that the force would be headed by an airman who had graduated from the Naval Academy. Lieutenant Yukio Seki had arrived from Formosa a month ago. He was their choice. Tamai called for Lieutenant Seki.

Seki was already asleep upstairs but soon came down and entered the officers' lounge. Tamai and Seki sat down together on one side of the table, Inoguchi, on the other. Tamai took Seki by the shoulder and told him about Onishi's proposal. Then he said, "Well, Seki, would you become commander of the First Special Attack Corps?" Tamai looked into Lieutenant Seki's eyes; they held tears.

Seki lowered his face and kept silent for a while as if he were considering. He had left his wife, to whom he had been married only a few months, back in Japan. With both elbows on the table, he quietly ran his hand through his long hair. Then he raised his face and said calmly, "Please let me do it."

Tamai and Inoguchi made a deep nod to each other and watched Seki with tears in his own eyes.

They consulted on a name for the corps and obtained the name Shinpu Unit at the suggestion of Inoguchi. Shinpu is also read as kamikaze, meaning divine wind. This was the name given the hurricanes, believed to have been divine interventions, that destroyed both Mongol invasions of Japan in 1274 and 1281.

Though it was late, Inoguchi visited the room of Vice Admiral Onishi and reported that twenty-four pilots had instantly volunteered for the Special Attack Force and that Lieutenant Seki had been chosen for commander.

Onishi, who had not slept but simply lain down on a temporary bed, only nodded in the dark of the room where the electric lights had been turned off. Vice Admiral Takijiro Onishi had been one of the pioneer advocates of the supremacy of air power in naval warfare, and along with Admiral Isoroku Yamamoto he had rejected the principal of the big gunship as out of date. He had clearly foreseen the defeat of Japan by the U.S. Air Force and had known of the poor production ability of the aircraft industry in Japan. If the war were to proceed as it was going now, in the near future the Japanese mainland would be under heavy attack by the Americans. He thought that there was nothing to prevent this but suicide tactics. Visiting the front lines, he had found this conclusion supported by what he saw. The difference in the number of planes compared to the American forces was too great, and airplane fuel was declining in quality, preventing aircraft from reaching their full performance. The skill of young pilots was low. They took off to intercept but were easy targets for American fighters.

The First Shinpu Special Attack Corps consisted of four units, all commanded by Lieutenant Seki; the units were headed by pilots Shikishima, Yamato, Asahi, and Yamazakura.

On the twenty-first of October, Onishi made a speech to the group's twenty-four members. "I beg you to do this for the nation. There is nothing but your spirits dying for the country to save it from this crisis. All the forces will surely follow you." Onishi's face was stiff, his body slightly shaking, and his eyes were full of tears.

At nine o'clock on the morning of that day, a signal came from a patrol plane: "Enemy task force in sight." The Special Attack Corps sallied out for the first time. But Lieutenant Seki's Zeros could not locate the American ships because of bad weather. Seki was very sorry he could not discover the enemy and apologized to Tamai in tears.

This situation was repeated three times. Then, on the twenty-fifth of October, the Shikishima unit under Lieutenant Seki found and attacked an American unit and never came back to its base.

Seki's unit, escorted by four other Zeros, consisted of Iwao Nakano, flying petty officer first class; Nobuo Tani, flying petty officer first class; Hajime Nagamine, flying warrant officer; and Shigeo Oguro, chief flying warrant officer. The planes carried 250-kilogram bombs. They made their crash attack at 10:45 A.M. through antiaircraft fire coming up at them like a heavy rain. They sank one aircraft carrier and a cruiser and caused a great fire on another aircraft carrier.

The heroic crash attack by aircraft, the kamikaze, one of the distinguishing features of the war between Japan and the United States, started that day. It continued on October 26 and 27. The scale gradually became larger.

To the young pilots ready to die this way, the crash attack became a day to day matter. No special thing about it arose. The tactic adopted by the navy quickly spread to the army pilots. Airplanes became a kind of bomb with a youth aboard. The Pacific Ocean became a grand suicidal place for youth who wanted to save their country from crisis. They were the victims of incapable war leaders, and they were also engulfed in the uncanny mouth of the huge monster which was the war.

Kamikaze attacks became a great menace to the American navy. The damage to ships was great, and the terror even greater. Some men even became insane and kept on muttering "kamikaze, kamikaze."

To counter these suicidal attacks the Americans increased their capacity for antiaircraft fire and interception by aircraft. Approaching planes would be caught in the American ships' radar network and many fighters would be launched to intercept. The fighters would surround the Japanese aircraft, slow to move because of the bombs they carried, and down them with concentrated machine gun fire. The numbers of kamikaze planes failing to reach a target rose greatly.

The miserable defeat in the Philippine Islands had completely cut off the supply route from the south to the Japanese mainland. It also permitted the American front line to come closer to the Japanese mainland. From that time, the Americans, who had completed the construction of airfields for heavy bombers, began to bomb the Japanese mainland.

The B-29 was developed for raiding Japan. It was assumed that its operational radius had to be about 2,800 kilometers. Its operational altitude was 9,000 meters. For the Japanese to intercept the B-29s, they had to have fighters able to operate at high altitudes; but there were few of these. The modified Reppu was still in development. Shusui, a joint development by the army and navy, was far from mass production. Shusui was a copy of the German Messerschmitt Me-163-B interceptor and was the first Japanese rocket fighter. It was designed by Mijiro Takahashi of the Nagoya Aircraft Works. He was chief designer. Others on his team were Tetsuro Hikita, Shunichi Sadamori, Nobu Kuroiwa, Toshihiko Narahara, and others. But even the number one test production model had not been completed by the time the B-29 air raids started.

What was available for defense were the army's Type 3 fighter (code name: Tony), the Type 2 single-seat fighter, the Type 1 fighter, the Type 2 two-seat fighter (code name: Nick), and the navy's Raiden, Shinden (code name: George), and Gekko (code name: Irving). But all of them could hardly maintain an altitude of 10,000 meters. If they banked at that height they would rapidly slide and lose the altitude. Interception of bombers, then, had to be limited to the first strike only. A second strike against the same target was impossible. As for intercepting at night, because of the poor radar system, that had to be limited to attacking only those B-29s caught in the searchlights.

Antiaircraft fire was also poor against B-29s operating at such high altitudes. At first, antiaircraft artillery units had been equipped with seven-centimeter antiaircraft cannons. They were effective up to 7,000 meters, but could not at all reach to the operational height of a B-29. Then antiaircraft guns of eight-centimeters and then twelve-centimeters were positioned. But because of poor radar they could not be effective against B-29s flying above the cloud or at night.

The attack of the B-29s from Saipan on the Japanese mainland was heralded by two reconnaissance planes that appeared over the Kanto area on November 1. The real attacks started on November 24 with a seventy-plane raid on Tokyo.

With the loss of Saipan Island, the Imperial General Headquarters had predicted air raids on Japan. In summer, they began forced evacuation of primary school children and recommended the evacuation of the citizens of big cities. They also ordered munitions factories to be scattered in the big cities. The Nagoya Aircraft Works was among those the forces said must move out.

Moving out, however, meant a severe decline in production, and the works were still having trouble deciding about this when the B-29 raids started. They made it definite that Nagoya works would be raided and the problem of moving the factories began to be seriously discussed. Some of the factories were then dispersed in and out of Nagoya.

Even with the disturbances of moving factories and air raids, 115 Zero fighters were produced in November 1944. That was thirty less than in October. But now the shortage of materials had also become more serious, and it had become more difficult to secure parts. The military, however, ignoring these conditions, demanded an increase in production. Of all things in the situation at the Nagoya works, only the demands for higher rates of production increased. The production required by the army and navy in 1944 was 10,259 planes. By the end of the year Nagoya works had made only 3,628, one third of the demand. And even those were produced only by the workers over-working. The production capability had come to its limits.

With the Americans getting close to the mainland, the military became extremely insistent about getting more aircraft, even by so much as one more. Their desire became a serious frustration to the companies and their workers. Things got to the point where an important staffer of a company was actually beaten by an officer because the man mentioned that the tremendous demands for production were unacceptable. And at the Nagoya works, staff at the inspectors office stationed at the company prohibited the evacuation of workers even for an air raid warning.

This was a serious objection. It was certain that the Nagoya works would be a major target of raids and to stay in the factory would be extremely dangerous. The inspectors, however, were afraid of losing production even during a raid. They were very strict about it, too. Once it happened that a warrant officer, stationed outside the fence, cut at the hands of workers climbing it in an effort to find refuge. For a remedy, the inspectors ordered Mitsubishi to dig shelters within the factory. That way, workers did not have to leave the works.

Even under these conditions, the devotion of the workers to their tasks continued. They labored with bloodshot eyes and wore head bands printed with a Rising Sun and the characters "kamikaze." The shortage of food, however, was leading to weakness, and many were those who had to leave due to illness.

For the oxen hauling the airplanes along with the Percheron horses to Kagamigahara, the situation was more miserable. Their feed mixture of wheat and sweet potato vine was being degraded as the ratio of wheat became smaller and smaller. Gradually, the animals were losing stamina. Many oxen stopped when hauling carts and did not move until they were beaten. They became miserable bags of bones.

Their steps became shaky, and some were found cold and dead in the morning.

The Percheron horses were also affected by the feed shortage. Day by day their thick coats lost their shine. Their stout bodies began to get thin. Sometimes they became exhausted midway on the journey to Kagamigahara and had to be changed. But there was still no other method to haul the planes.

Twenty-one

On the afternoon of December 7, 1944, a sudden uncanny sound from the ground made the air of Nagoya vibrate. Instantly the ground began to heave. It was a great earthquake.

The Nagoya Aircraft Works had been built on reclaimed land, and so the shaking was particularly violent. The buildings of the factory heaved with a crashing sound. The disturbance in the works was tremendous. Workers trying to escape out of the buildings could not even keep their feet. Some crawled under things, others ran out of the buildings, reeling on the trembling earth. Screams sounded. It seemed the bottoms of the buildings had broken. Sand and water burst out of them. Many cracks spread over concrete floors. Everywhere, buildings began to fall down with great noise.

The shaking at last began to calm, but there were still many strong aftershocks. Each time buildings collapsed. The works was turned into a wretched sight. The damage was especially heavy at the Dotoku factory which had been moved to the Dotoku area within the city as part of the dispersion. The factory had belonged to the Nisshin Spinning Factory. Here the Type 100 reconnaissance plane was assembled. The frame assembly and parts sections of the factory had completely collapsed. The roof of the heat processing section and store had fallen in completely.

Among the worst damage was that to the frame assembly factory, which was made of bricks. Those working there had no time to get out of the building. At the sudden shock, they had crowded along a brick wall, hoping for shelter. They got the opposite. The bricks were old. The wall fell down and crushed many people under it.

Even while the aftershocks went on, workers from the works started to remove the bricks. The place had turned into a heap of rubble and gravel filled with moans and blood. Then human bodies began to appear from under the bricks. Many alive had bones crushed, their skin torn open, and their flesh exposed. The corpses of women wearing *monpe* trousers and head bands and those of high school students, too, in their uniforms, were successively dug out. The sun set. With all the electricity in the city cut, darkness covered the area. By the light of lanterns, the removal of rubble and gravel went on. The figures of many girl students could be seen among the rescuers, removing bricks with bloody hands and calling the names of friends.

Those severely wounded were carried to the Mitsubishi hospital on stretchers or doors. Corpses were laid on straw mats in the lecture hall of the youth school. The corpses were severely mangled. Many faces and bodies were completely crushed and hard to distinguish. By the words of their comrades, or by the families who came in haste, the bodies were identified one by one.

Midnight came. Two people had not yet been found. By lantern light, the search proceeded. At last, near dawn, the crushed remains of a high school student and a worker were found. That ended the recovering of corpses.

Many died after they had been carried to the hospital. The final count of those killed at the Dotoku factory was fifty-nine, including boy and girl high school students. Seventy-two people had been severely wounded. Numerous others were wounded lightly. At other factories, one transportation worker had been instantly killed at the second storehouse of the Oe main factory; and at the Kuwana factory, moved to Kuwana City in the dispersion, one student of Ueno High School had been crushed to death by a brick chimney. At the Harisaki factory, six people, including two girl students, were killed. Altogether the quake killed sixty-eight.

The damage to the works was heavy. Besides those buildings that had collapsed, many others were weakened. They could not be approached because of the danger of collapse. And many buildings fortunate enough to survive without collapse, lost much of their capacity for airplane manufacture.

A very serious loss was the assembly jig that provided the standard for assembling airframes. This had gotten out of alignment because the floor had distorted, and it could not be used again without a precise check. Elsewhere, floors had been covered with mud and water that burst up from broken and sunken floors. Pillars had been weakened, and all the glass windows were smashed. Many parts of ceilings had fallen in. It seemed it would take days to repair the damage.

The army was asked to help in reactivating the works. All efforts concentrated on reopening production, starting with the recovery of the jigs. At the same time, it was decided to carry out the dispersal of the works. The Dotoku factory, which had been destroyed, was to be moved to a region far away.

Then on the eighteenth of December, eleven days after the earthquake, came another, of equal calamity. About noon on that day, B-29 bombers approached, flying in a straight line from the direction of the Chita Peninsula. Long vapor trails came from them. Numerous bombs came out of their bodies and fell into the Nagoya Aircraft Works like a heavy rain.

Instantly the works and surrounding areas were engulfed by the great sound, like that of a volcanic explosion. Many splinters flew high into the sky. Other groups of B-29s appeared, one by one. They scattered something glittering in the clear blue winter sky. Fires broke out within the works. The buildings were mercilessly destroyed. The sky became covered in smoke from the fires.

At last the B-29s were gone. Workers who had survived the calamity came out of the shelters and were struck dumb by the state of the works. The office building, the second manufacturing section and main office, and forty other buildings had been destroyed. Fires raged everywhere.

They tried to extinguish the fires and then discovered that the loss of human life in the raid had been heavy. Damage to the factories of the first manufacturing section, where the naval fighters were made, was particularly bad. Among them the wing factory had been the target of concentrated bombing.

The heavy casualties had obviously occurred because most of the workers had stayed within the factories during the raid. Most of their air raid shelters within the factories had been destroyed. Some had been hit directly and were obliterated. Bloody pieces of human bodies were everywhere in the factories.

After carrying out the injured, the recovery of corpses began. There were grisly sights—eyeballs popped out of heads or organs blown out of a body by the blast. There were corpses lacking limbs and a head. Limbs were to be found all over the works. Some were even caught in the beams or electric wires. Those engaged in recovering bodies were at a loss at what to do with the pieces of bodies. They decided to gather them in the lecture hall of the school without trying to identify them.

As night fell, the last corpse was collected. But the scraping of flesh attached to unfinished wings, or pillars and walls went on.

About nine in the evening, the vice director of the works, Yoshito Yoshida, entered the lecture hall followed by Kenji Murakami, the welfare supervisor of the labor section. Together they directed the arrangement of the bodies. They made a list of those lost and then tried to distinguish the bodies from it. Almost none of the corpses was perfectly intact. Even those identified often lacked limbs or heads. Gradually the number of corpses identified increased. Those identified were laid out in regular rows of straw mats. About one third of the bodies remained difficult to distinguish. They kept trying to fit dismembered parts to the bodies, but it was hard. Family members made rough identifications.

The school where the identification process was going on had students from a wide area—from Tohoku in the north to Kyushu in the south. The dismembered remains of workers from those areas could not be identified, with families living so far away. With no other choice, these remains were finally cremated together and the ashes divided evenly.

The raid had killed 215 people and severely wounded 208. Half of them were drafted workers, labor service students, and women volunteers.

Condolence money was paid at the standard rate to family members, workers, and drafted workers. The company gave about 5,000 yen to the students. The Minister of Munitions, the director of the General Bureau of Aerial Weapons, and the chief of the Munition

Control Department only gave ten yen each as an offering to the ghosts of the departed. The bodies and ashes remaining were to be held by their families.

The air raid, coming on the heels of a major earthquake, almost knocked out the Nagoya works. It forced the military and the company's leaders to face the reality that production was going to have to stop while a general and very necessary dispersal of the works took place. How this could be done depended on the opinions of the heads of the manufacturing sections, Shunichi Yajima, chief of the first manufacturing section, where naval planes were made; Naoichi Yui, his assistant; Totaro Arikawa, head of the second manufacturing section, maker of army planes; and Gakuji Moriya, his assistant.

They waited to respond to a dispersal plan devised by the research section, specially appointed to figure out the dispersal. It was headed by Yoichiro Makita. He was assisted by Raizo Wakasugi, the section's supervisor, and other members of the section. Their task was urgent. The dispersal had to be carried out as soon as possible so production could resume.

The most urgent requirement of the military was for the Type 100 reconnaissance plane that had been in production at the completely destroyed Dotoku factory. It was an excellent plane, the fastest among all the army and navy planes. The military wanted it produced on an emergency basis. First however, the Dotoku factory had to be moved.

The first task was to find new locations. Wakasugi, the supervisor, went to the Hokuriku district in haste and managed to borrow the factories of Kureha Spinning in Daimon town, Imizu County, Toyama Prefecture, for two years. Production facilities for the Type 100 reconnaissance plane were moved there. Altogether they formed the Hokuriku area, absorbing the Fukuno and Inami spinning factories in the neighborhood and the Yamato Aircraft Factory and Daiken Industry in Kanazawa. The whole complex was called the Eleventh Works.

For the move, a transportation corps was formed specially, under the Minister of Munitions. Many railway tracks were used, and freight cars were assigned priority. Several hundred soldiers were assigned to the rush work of removing spinning machines or rearranging factories. By the end of the year, production had started at the dispersed factories.

The design section was moved to Matsumoto, where it used the Katakura Spinning Factory or schools nearby. It was called the First

Works. Here, Yoshitoshi Sone, who had become chief designer, since Horikoshi was again on his sickbed, continued the development of the Reppu and its successors. Tomio Kubo meanwhile worked on the development of the army's long-range, twin-engine fighter, the Ki-83.

For the production of the army's Type 4 heavy bomber (Hiryu) the Fifth Works was formed out of dispersed factories in Nagano and Ofu in Chita County, Aichi Prefecture. The works stood beside the Kumamoto Aircraft Works (called the Ninth Works). The Mizushima Aircraft Works made the Type 1 land-based torpedo bomber and Shiden-Kai fighter. They were renamed the Seventh Works.

The production facilities for the Zero were dispersed to spinning factories in Suzuka in Mie Prefecture, and also in Kuwana, Yokaichi, and Tsu, and in the Omi or Nankai areas. They were called the Third Works. These works also had produced the Type 1 torpedo bomber and the Raiden, made in the existing Suzuka maintenance factory.

So the Nagoya Aircraft Works were completely split up after the damage caused by the earthquake and air raid.

Since their start in 1945, the B-29 air raids had become more intense with every passing day. By the end of February, about 1,100 B-29s had dropped bombs in great quantity upon mainly military facilities and munitions factories. Meanwhile, on February 19th, the Americans, completely dominating the Japanese forces, starting landing on Iwo Jima.

Iwo Jima lay between the island of Saipan and Tokyo. If the Americans could construct step airfields on it, all of Japan would come within range of the B-29s. With the island holding such importance, the garrison of 23,000 on Iwo planned a ferocious resistance.

Against them, the Americans committed an enormous quantity of materials. An endless bombardment by about sixty fighting ships took place while 1,600 carrier planes per day strafed and bombed, transforming the landscape. The Japanese troops, however, kept on fighting with their poor weapons. The injured did not retreat from their posts. Many soldiers holding explosives dived at tanks. They killed or injured 33,000 American troops, destroyed 270 tanks, and still kept up a desperate fight. They suffered, however, the fate of all the other isolated Japanese garrisons. Their positions were obliterated. They ran out of ammunition and most of the soldiers were killed in action.

Lieutenant General Tadamichi Kuribayashi, the divisional commander, sent his last message on March 17. "Tonight I will lead a general charge of all left. We pray for victory and the safety of the Empire." Then a shock assault of the last 800 soldiers left was made on the American positions. All died.

The fall of Iwo Jima was directly reflected in an increase in the scale of air raids by B-29s. During March, more than 1,000 planes made raids. Formations used to be of 100 aircraft, but now they grew to 170. On the night of March 9, they began the awesome firebombing of Tokyo. The bombing was indiscriminate, with the aim of massacring the ordinary people and destroying their daily life.

The bombing tactic was to drop fire bombs so as to surround the region of the target area and seal off escape. Then great quantities of fire bombs would be sprinkled on block after block. The city became engulfed in a firestorm in no time, and citizens, unable to escape, were incinerated.

Then, on February 26, the first raid by carrier aircraft and fighters from Iwo Jima came—1,200 planes in all. They roved all over the Japanese mainland, freely strafing and bombing.

On the morning of that day, the sea around the Okinawa Islands in Japan was covered with more than 1,000 American ships, forming a great iron circle. At 8 A.M. transports launched numerous landing craft, and trailing many wakes, they rushed in to the Kadena shore in the middle of the island. The size of the landing group was 183,000, against a garrison on Okinawa of 60,000. A desperate battle began, led on the Japanese side by Lieutenant General Mitsuru Ushijima.

The American troops landed and headed south without encountering much resistance until they reached the main Japanese defense line five kilometers north of Shuri, which held the Japanese headquarters. The battle then became hard and ferocious over every inch of ground.

Day after day the great American fleet surrounding the islands rained down tens of thousands of shells on the Japanese positions. From above, more thousands of carrier aircraft kept up a steady strafing and bombing. The Japanese soldiers hid in caves or grave holes and at night repeated the grand-scale shock charge and secured their positions. They were encouraged by the cooperation of the people of Okinawa, who risked their lives trying to defend their land. Men of over seventeen and under forty-five formed a defense troop. Boys from high school formed the Troop for the Emperor with Iron and

Blood and joined the army as privates. Girls in high school and others joined the army as special nurses. The Japanese soldiers jumped beneath the caterpillar tracks of American tanks holding handmade bombs. High school boys, holding bamboo lances, charged shouting at the American positions.

However, the American troops, supported by the bombardment of warships and planes, kept on advancing inch by inch, using tanks as their shield. They poured gasoline into caves and set them alight. They used flamethrowers. If resistance continued, they drilled holes into the rock and threw in a quantity of explosives.

At last, Shuri fell. It had been a terrible battle. In spite of their tremendous power, the Americans had taken eighty days to cover the five kilometers from the first defense line to Shuri. The American troops who captured Shuri cornered the remaining Japanese troops in the south of the island. Civilians were also with the troops, trapped in a small area facing the sea.

The morale of the American troops rose more and more, and they kept up a merciless attack. They asked the Japanese to surrender, but the soldiers and high school students kept on charging defiantly. Young women or old people committed suicide to avoid capture. And on June 23, Lieutenant General Mitsuru Ushijima and other garrison leaders killed themselves, either by the traditional method of disembowelment or by revolver. The battle of Okinawa had ended.

About 75,000 Japanese troops, including members of the defense force and the students' Troop for the Emperor with Iron and Blood, died in action. In addition, 85,500 civilians had died. American casualties were 49,000, including 11,400 killed in action. Lieutenant General Buckner, the commander of the American troops, was also killed in the battle.

In this battle, an unusual number of American troops became insane. It was because of the tremendous numbers of Japanese special attack aircraft cooperating with the garrison. They dived without respite into the American ships around Okinawa.

This was the special attack operation called Kikusui (meaning Floating Chrysanthemums—the symbol of a warlord loyal to the emperor). The operation started with an attack by 699 army and navy planes (including 355 planes for the Special Attack Corps) on April 6 and 7. A great number of special attack planes from Kyushu and Formosa followed after.

These attacks caused much damage to the ships and created great disturbances among the troops. Admiral Raymond Spruance, the commander in chief of the Fifth Fleet, was very concerned about these attacks and asked Admiral Chester Nimitz, commander in chief of the Pacific Fleet, for air raids on the bases of the special attack planes on Formosa and Kyushu. Kerama anchorage near Okinawa was filled with damaged ships. Warnings of special attack planes horrified American soldiers. They would put a defensive fire over their ships that left no gaps. But the special attack planes passed through anyway and plunged into the warships or transports, blowing up.

Terrified by these attacks, the Americans tried many countermeasures. First of all, answering to the demands of Admiral Spruance, 300 B-29s and 1,650 carrier aircraft attacked the special attack plane bases on Kyushu. The Americans also reconstructed the airfields on Okinawa and used them, while the carriers withdrew from the range of kamikaze attack. They also set great numbers of fighters to intercepting the special attack craft. There were other measures too. The Americans could decipher the code of the Japanese forces and knew their plans, and their superior radar made detection of incoming Japanese aircraft fairly certain.

These obstacles were enough trouble for the special attack forces to face. In addition, however, planes of excellent performance were just about all used up. The Japanese air force had been completely weakened. For special attacks, all planes, even those lacking any fighting capability, were used. Many training planes were modified to carry bombs. In addition, pilots were poor in flying skills, in spite of their strong desire to save their country from crisis. It was extremely difficult to avoid the swarming American fighters. As a result, the chance of successfully reaching a target went down with each attack.

A steady stream of miscellaneous Japanese planes flown by unskilled pilots and with bombs attached sallying forth to Okinawa over the sea—it was a sight that came to symbolize the Japanese in the Pacific War.

On June 25, the Imperial General Headquarters officially announced the end of the battle of Okinawa. During that gruesome fight, 7,852 Japanese army and navy aircraft made sorties against American ships. The special attack aircraft among them numbered 1,439 navy and 954 army planes. Many pilots were lost with their planes. The Americans had 404 ships sunk or damaged, and many American soldiers were killed.

The battle for Okinawa ended with the defeat of the Japanese, but it had cost the Americans more than three months to capture the island and postponed plans for the invasion of the mainland. The ferocious resistance both of the garrison and the people of Okinawa horrified the Americans and made them more prudent about plans to attack the mainland.

The mainland they were planning to attack had already been turned into a wretched sight by the B-29s and the carrier aircraft. In June, B-29 raids came to 3,270. Carrier aircraft raids came to 4,312. Bombing, mainly with fire bombs, of medium and even small cities was indiscriminate. Increasingly, ordinary citizens were casualties and their daily lives destroyed.

Rations, already scarce, began to be delayed. People began to fear they would starve. Necessities for living could not be obtained anywhere. In ragged clothes, those threatened by air raid huddled at night in bomb shelters amid fire-blackened ruins. Still, most people prayed for victory for Japan, and kept on working in the munitions factories, driving their wasted bodies to one more effort.

Ordinary people did not know that by now, Japan's industrial strength had been lost, and that the production capability of every industry had shrunk to a shocking extent. Military policy had concentrated all of Japan's national industrial strength into the munitions industry. But even in this area, production had rapidly declined to 35 percent for steel and nonferrous metals, 24 percent for liquid fuel, and 27 percent for shipbuilding, compared to the period of maximum production during the war. The production of necessities for living, sacrificed for munitions, had declined so terribly that life for ordinary people had been made impossible. There was only 2 percent of cotton fabrics, 2 percent of woolen cloth, and zero percent of leather shoes, edible oil, and sugar available compared with production in 1937.

In this situation, the production of Zero fighters at the Nagoya Aircraft Works declined rapidly. The works had made fifty-nine Zeros in February 1945, forty in March, thirty-eight in May, and twenty-three in June, compared with 145 in October of 1944. The production of the Type 1 land-based torpedo bomber was even bleaker: eleven in April, five in May, three in June, and none in July. Sixteen Raiden were produced in April, none in May, and eight in June.

Conditions were the same at the dispersed factories producing other kinds of planes or engines. Worse, as the air raids on small cities

became heavier, it became necessary to disperse the dispersed factories again. But American planes were always flying above, carefully
scouting. New locations for factories had to be where they could not
be seen from above. Underground or semi-underground factories were
required.

To meet this necessity, the construction of factories built like tunnels, semi-underground and semi-cylindrical and covered with soil had
begun. Tunnels that could also be useful were surveyed. One example
was the tunnel of the national highway at Kannonzaka in Shiga Prefecture. Machine tools were carried in and then the tunnel sealed at
both ends. In a mine that produced polishing sand, a gallery was turned
into a machine factory. Tunnel factories were under construction in
haste everywhere.

The dispersion of the factories made the supply of parts desperately difficult. Traffic was often blocked. Trucks had no gasoline. Tele-
phone lines were cut everywhere, and letters often failed to arrive.
Inevitably, the delivery of parts came to depend on humans carrying
rucksacks. They departed in groups with their packs to pick up parts.
Troublesome procedures were necessary to take the train. Those that
finally got onto the train had to endure overcrowding on their way to
a far destination. At the destination, they desperately hunted up the
parts, pushed them in the rucksacks and returned to the factory, without delay, night or day. They were called the rucksack troops, and at
every factory, those carrying rucksacks were busily kept on the go.

In this situation, the Suzuka maintenance factory for the last stage
of assembly for the Zero and others had miraculously escaped damage by air raid. The factory employed 8,000, but half were drafted
workers, students, and women volunteers. They devoted themselves
to the work as much as the regular workers. They willingly volunteered for the hard task of carrying parts in rucksacks and did not go
home even late at night, when the foreman said they could. High school
girls with *monpe* trousers and disheveled hair worked overtime
throughout the night. They volunteered for riveting and without a
word handled the heavy riveting machines. In spite of all these efforts, however, only fifteen fighters were made at Mitsubishi in July.

The completed Zeros were carried out of the factory and pushed
along the way about 1,000 meters to the Suzuka Airfield by the women
volunteers and the girl students. The Suzuka Mountains could be seen
far away and from their left came the croak of frogs in the paddy

fields there. Workers and girls often patted the airframe they were pushing.

A sole Zero fighter moving through the paddy fields, pushed by women. It was a sad sight, in striking contrast to the activity in the days when many airframes advanced along the assembly line to the sound of a bugle. But in this situation, workers and girls felt more affection for the Zero fighter that had been completed at last.

It was considered only a matter of time before the American forces would start landing on the mainland. Having totally lost their fighting power, the Japanese army and navy insisted on do-or-die resistance, and prepared for this with all the resources left. The heart of the resistance operation was to be the general special attack.

The army and navy were planning to modify all airplanes, including reconnaissance planes, bombers, and trainers—more than half the planes left in the country—into kamikaze aircraft. They were to crash into the American ships. There were also specially designed special attack planes in production: the Oka (code name: Baka), the Shinryu, and the Tsurugi. The Oka was a rocket-propelled gliding bomb launched from a parent plane. The Shinryu, another rocket plane, launched from the ground. The Tsurugi was strictly for suicide attack—its undercarriage could be jettisoned after takeoff. They were all manned bombs on a one-way mission, and training for the soldiers to pilot them had commenced. To the forces, the pilot was no longer human but merely a device for controlling the bomb.

On the sea, five kinds of special attack vessel were prepared: the Kairyu, the Koryu, the Kaiten, the Shinyo, and the Fukuryu. Training for these went on with the few destroyers and submarines left. All of them were specialized, there was no hope of return. The Fukuryu was an especially primitive man-mine. It was a soldier equipped with a scuba and hiding in the sea with the mine attached to a shaft. When a landing craft passed above, he would push the mine against the hull of the landing craft. Of course he would be killed in the blast.

These special attack planes and vessels were positioned along the Pacific coast, mainly at Kyushu. The Japanese mainland was about to turn into an Armageddon in which would be sacrificed the old and women and children. Already more than 2,600,000 soldiers and civilians had been killed; the crippled filled the towns.

The sky above Japan became filled with American planes. The B-29 raids reached 33,000. The raids of carrier planes and other aircraft reached twice that number. And there were warships bombarding the shores, too. Almost 200,000 tons of bombs and shells fell on the country. Ninety-six cities and towns were incinerated. Of those, seventy-two had no military facilities of importance. This was evidence that the purpose of the raids was mainly to demoralize the ordinary citizen. Death had already claimed a toll of 400,000 ordinary citizens. Famine stalked the cities that had been reduced to ashes.

This thoroughly indiscriminate bombing reached its climax and exposed even more the horrible reality of war in the atomic bombing of Hiroshima on August 6 and Nagasaki on the ninth. In those cities, 260,000 citizens were killed instantly.

Over the radio U.S. President Harry Truman gave a warning to Japan after the bombing of Hiroshima. "The atomic bomb that was dropped on Hiroshima has revolutionized the war. If Japan does not surrender, it will be dropped on other cities." And as he said, the second one fell on Nagasaki.

Even in this situation the military insisted on do-or-die resistance. However, the appearance of a weapon whose sole purpose was to massacre civilians suppressed even the most manic voices and brought an end to the war.

August fifteenth. . . .

The sky was clear, but to no purpose. Under the sun, workers, drafted workers, students, and women volunteers lined up reverently and listened to the voice of the Emperor mingled with static on the radio. The broadcast ended quickly.

A deep lethargy and weariness came over the faces of all the listeners, who remained standing in line. Then, the soft sobs of girls started, and in no time it spread to workers and boy students. They had learned that all their efforts had been in vain. They had not imagined this result. The only comfort was the thought that they had worked to the extent of their strength.

The number of Zero fighters produced at Mitsubishi in August before the war ended was six. The line broke up and they looked vacantly at the assembly factory. The fuselages and wings for twelve Zeros stood drearily there.

In the evening of that day, Vice Admiral Matome Ugaki, the commander in chief of the Fifth Air Fleet, sallied forth in a Suisei carrier-borne bomber (code name: Judy) from the air base at Oita to make a crash attack on American ships off Okinawa's main island (the official order to cease operations had not yet arrived from the combined fleet). He intended to take responsibility for the many youths he had driven to their death. Flying Warrant Officer Akifumu Endo, who was in the back seat of the Suisei, was dragged out of the plane by Ugaki. But he begged to be taken and squeezed in the same seat as Ugaki. Nine bombers headed by Lieutenant Tatsuo Nakatsuru followed him. Lieutenant Jinroku Kaneko, who was charged with confirming the results of the mission, loaded his Saiun, a carrier-borne reconnaissance plane (code name: Myrt) with a torpedo and also took off to make a crash attack. However, the leading plane Ugaki had boarded was shot down by American interceptors and none of the others reached the target area.

On the morning of the next day, August 16, Vice Admiral Onishi, chief of the naval general staff and the one who had planned and carried out the first attack by the special attack corps at the battle of Leyte, disembowelled himself. It is said that his agony was long, but he refused medical treatment or mercy killing.

The hot, late summer days were over and an autumn wind began to blow.

One day in the afternoon, Seiichiro Tamura, the chief of the transportation system at the Nagoya works, was standing with several people from transport companies including the Onishi company in the burned-out remains of the Oe main factory. Percheron horses, coated with long hair, were huddled in front of them. Each was poking its head into a manger.

All the oxen had died from insufficient fodder and hard work. The Percheron horses had also died, one by one. Out of eighty-nine, fifteen barely survived. Tamura had gathered the horses that were now busily eating fodder. They had changed so much it was almost impossible to imagine their figures, once so substantial, and the magnificent tireless way the Percherons had towed the carts. They were surprisingly thin now. Under their skin, covered with discolored hair, their great frames could easily be seen.

Naojiro Okano, the director of the works, had told Tamura to distribute these horses to the Onishi company and others.

When the horses had finished eating, Tamura handed the bridles of the Percherons one by one to the people of the companies gathered with him. "Please take good care of them," he said, in a hoarse voice.

Then the horses had gone through the burned-out gate of the factory, guided by their new owners. Tamura went out onto the road and
saw them off. At each step, the bones of the horses could be seen
moving under their skin. With heavy steps, they went away along the
deserted road through the burned-out ruins.

Standing very still, Tamura desperately resisted the impulse to
sob. The wind was blowing, and the only sound was the rattling of
burned tin plate.

Index

About the Author and Translators

AKIRA YOSHIMURA is a specialist at the "technohistory." Born in Tokyo in 1927, he started to write while a student at Gakushuin University. He has published over 50 books, many of them technohistories. *Zero Fighter* was a best seller in Japan, selling over 300,000 copies.

RETSU KAIHO is a senior officer with the Japan Defense Agency and an expert in aeronautics.

MICHAEL GREGSON did a rewrite of the English translation started by Kaiho; he is a technical editor living in Victoria, British Columbia, Canada.